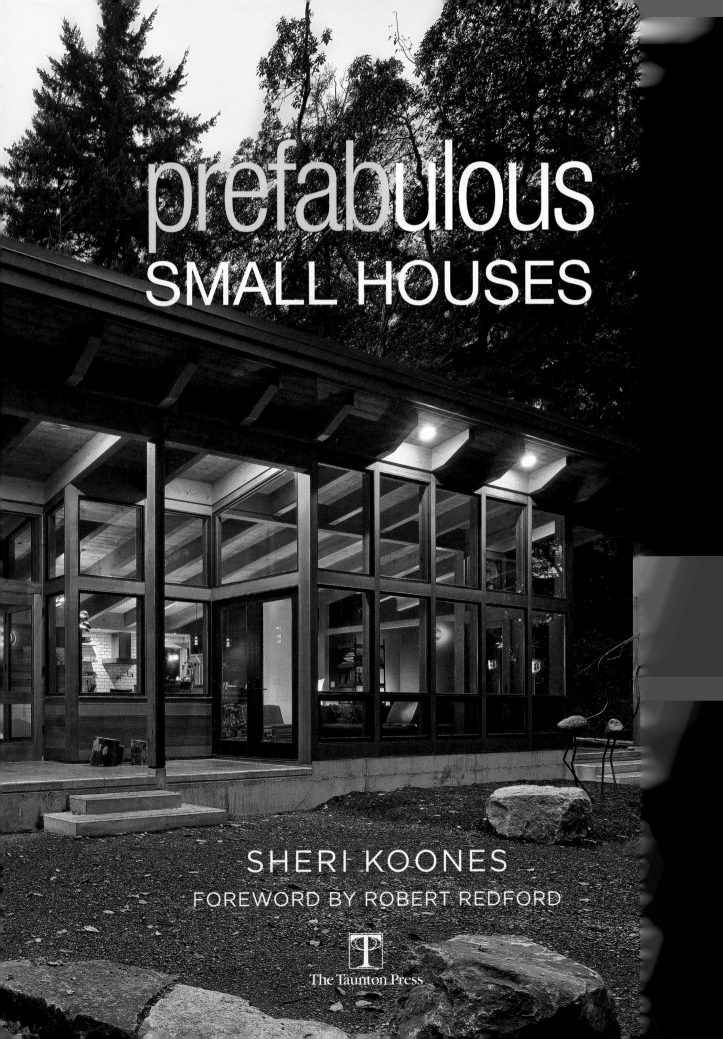

prefabulous
SMALL HOUSES

SHERI KOONES
FOREWORD BY ROBERT REDFORD

The Taunton Press

The Taunton Press
Inspiration for hands-on living®

The Taunton Press, Inc.,
63 South Main Street, PO Box 5506,
Newtown, CT 06470-5506
Email: tp@taunton.com

Editors: Steve Culpepper, Peter Chapman
Copy Editor: Candace B. Levy
Illustrations: Charles Lockhart
Jacket/Cover, Interior design, and Layout: Rita Sowins / Sowins Design
Cover photo courtesy of Barta Pictures
Half title page photo courtesy of Trent Bell
Title page photo courtesy of Kevin Walsh Photography
Facing page photo courtesy of Joe Fletcher

The following names/manufacturers appearing in *Prefabulous Small Houses* are trademarks:
Advanced Energy®, AGEPAN®, Airbnb®, AIR-board®, Aire-Flo®, AirRenew®, Airstream®, American Clay®, American Forests® Americh®, Amerisips®, Andersen®, Ann Sacks®, Arcadia®, Armstrong®, Artemide®, AutoCAD®, Azek®, Bamboo Hardwoods®, Bartels®, Bega®, BendPak®, Benjamin Moore®, Bensonwood®, Big Ass Fans®, BioBricks®, B-K Lighting®, Blomberg®, Blown-In-Blanket®, Blu Homes®, BMW i3®, Bombard Renewable Energy®, Bosch®, Bristolite®, Brizo®, Broan®, Broan-NuTone®, Buderus®, Built Green™, Bushman™, C.H.I. Overhead Doors®, CALGreen®, Cali Bamboo®, Cambria®, Campbell®, Carlisle®, Ceasarstone®, Cem-Clad®, Centennial Woods™, CertainTeed®, Clarvista™, Clopay®, Cor-Ten®, Cradle to Cradle Certified™, Craigslist®, Cree®, Daikin®, Daltile®, Danze®, DensGlass®, Design within Reach®, Dornbracht®, Dow®, DuChâteau®, Dumpster®, Duravit®, Dwell®, Eagle®, eBay®, EchoPanel®, EcoBatt®, ECOLOGO®, EcoSmart™, EcoTimber®, EcoTop®, Elan®, Electrolux®, eMonitor™, ENERGY STAR®, Enphase Energy®, Essentia®, Excel Homes®, FabCab®, Faber®, Fagor®, Feeney®, Fireplace Xtrordinair®, Fischer & Paykel®, FLOR®, Florida Tile®, Folding Sliding Door Company®, Forest Stewardship Council®, Forms+Surfaces®, Frazee®, Frigidaire®, FSB®, Fujitsu®, Gaggenau®, Galvalume®, GE®, Geberit®, GeoSpring™, Gerkin™, Global ReLeaf®, Graham & Brown®, Green Depot®, GreenFab®, GREENGUARD™, Green Seal®, Grohe®, Grundfos®, Gurit®, Haas Cabinet®, Haiku®, Hansgrohn®, HDP High Definition Porcelain®, Heat & Glo®, Heatilator®, Herman Miller®, HERS®, HighVelocityHelper.com™, HI-MACS®, Hinkley®, Home Depot®, Houzer®, Hubbardton Forge®, IceStone®, Icynene®, Ignis®, IKEA®, Insteon®, Insulspan®, Integrity®, Irontown Homes®, Jacuzzi®, James Hardie®, Jeld-Wen®, Jenn-Air®, Juno®, Kallista®, Keiser®, Kentwood Floors™, Kim Lighting®, Kirei™, Knoll®, Kohler®, KWC®, Kynar®, LaHabra®, Lamboo®, Leadership in Energy and Environmental Design™, LEED Platinum®, LEED®, Lego®, LG Hausys®, LG TurboWash™, Liebherr®, LifeBreath®, LifeSource Water Systems®, Lightolier®, Ligne Roset®, Lindal®, Live Edge Design®, Loewen®, Logix®, Loll®, Louis Poulsen®, Luceplan®, Lumisplash®, Lutron®, Lyptus®, Ma(i)sonry®, Maax®, Majestic®, Marvin®, Merillat®, Metal Roofing Alliance®, Metal Sales™, Method Homes®, Metropolitan Appliance™, Microsoft® Surface™, Minka-Aire®, Miele®, Milgard®, Mitsubishi Electric®, Moen®, Morsø®, Moxie®, NAHB®, National Trust for Historic Preservation®, Navien®, Nest Learning Thermostat®, Nexia™, Noritz®, Novalis®, Oceanside Glasstile®, Open-Built®, OPTIMA®, Owens Corning®, Palm Harbor®, Panasonic®, PaverSearch™, PentelQuartz®, PGT®, Plastpro®, Plyboo®, Poggenpohl®, Premier SIPs®, Prescolite®, Pro Clima®, PureFlow®, RedBuilt™, Renusol®, Residential Energy Services Network® (RESNET®), Restoration Hardware®, Resysta®, Rheem®, Rich Brilliant Willing®, Richlite®, Rinnai®, Roche Bobois®, Roxul®, Ruud®, Sarnafil®, Schrock®, Schüco®, Schweitzer Engineering Laboratories®, SenseME™, Sharp®, Sheetrock®, Sherwin-Williams®, Sierra Pacific Window®, Siga®, Sika®, Silestone®, SiteSage®, Sliding Door Company®, SLV®, SMA®, Sto®, Styrofoam®, Sub-Zero®, Summit Appliance®, Sunbrella®, SunPower®, Teragren®, Thermador®, Therma-Tru®, Thermolec®, Thermomass®, Timberline®, TJI®, Toto®, Trane®, Trex®, TruGrain™, Trulite®, U. S. Steel®, U.S. Green Building Council®, UL®, Ultra-Aire™, Unico System®, Unilock®, USAI®, USFloors®, VaproShield®, Velux®, Venmar®, Vent-A-Hood®, Vermont Custom Cabinetry™, Viega®, Viessmann®, WAC Lighting®, Wagner™, Walker Zanger®, Watercycles™, WaterSense®, weeHouse®, West Elm®, Westech®, Wetstyle®, Whirlpool®, WhisperComfort™, WhisperGreen Select™, Wolf®, Wyndham Collection®

Library of Congress Cataloging-in-Publication Data

Names: Koones, Sheri, 1949- author.
Title: Prefabulous small houses / Sheri Koones ; foreword by Robert Redford.
Description: Newtown, CT : The Taunton Press, Inc., [2016]
Identifiers: LCCN 2016021033| ISBN 9781631864049 (hardcover) | ISBN
    9781631864414 (paperback)
Subjects: LCSH: Prefabricated houses. | Ecological houses. | Small houses. |
    Dwellings--Energy conservation. | Modular construction. | Architecture,
    Domestic--United States--Designs and plans.
Classification: LCC TH4819.P7 K659 2016 | DDC 728--dc23
LC record available at https://lccn.loc.gov/2016021033

Printed in the United States of America
10 9 8 7 6 5 4 3 2 1

FOR CHERE AND MARK, STILL FRIENDS AFTER ALL THESE YEARS

ACKNOWLEDGMENTS

I AM INDEBTED TO ALL OF THE PHOTOGRAPHERS, ARCHITECTS, BUILDERS, and manufacturers who shared their time, information, and photos. Thank you to the homeowners who graciously allowed me to profile their houses in this book.

Thank you to Steve Culpepper for an excellent editing job, to Chuck Lockhart for his beautiful graphics, and to Peter Chapman for his support in getting this book published.

A special thank you to Robert Redford for his enduring support for my books. He continues to inspire me with his important environmental work; he sets the bar high in his work protecting this planet and the future generations who will inhabit it. My love and gratitude to Alex, Jesse, and Rob for their ongoing support and encouragement of my work and to my extended family.

Sonoma Residence; photo courtesy of Joe Fletcher

CONTENTS

FOREWORD

BY ROBERT REDFORD

OVER THE LAST 30 YEARS, I've been engaged in trying to raise awareness on the issue of climate change. I never imagined decades later, I would be fighting the same battle.

After years of talk and political paralysis, we have reached a tipping point. Climate change is no longer a problem of the future—we are experiencing the results of a warming planet all around us in rising seas, widening deserts, and deadly wildfires. We are losing control of our future. Our civilization is threatened today by changes that have been taking place over decades.

Climate change affects everyone, in every country. Climate change is in everybody's backyard. Only by acting now and standing together can we tip the scales and achieve the results necessary to make the planet a healthy and safe place to live—for now and for the future. At one time energy conversation was about only oil, coal, and gas. Now people are talking about renewable energy—how it can result in cheaper and plentiful energy and the positive role this can play on the environment.

Climate change presents us with a huge challenge—how to move a society that has been dependent on fossil fuels to a future that is cleaner and more sustainable.

While it is easy to become discouraged, there is reason for optimism. There is a ground-swell occurring and it's rising from the ground up. Leadership is coming from people themselves. We have the opportunity to rethink how we live in this world now and for future generations.

I have great faith in the power of innovation and the ingenuity of people from all walks of life to solve this problem. Technological advances are well under way—renewable energy, increased efficiency, and innovation in building practices are gaining momentum.

One way to reduce the need and desire for fossil fuel is to design houses that require less fuel to build, operate, and heat and cool. When houses are thoughtfully built this way, the energy requirement is vastly reduced. Renewable energy that uses solar thermal panels, photovoltaic panels, wind turbines, and geothermal systems—combined with good design—creates houses that require no fossil fuel.

We know that 38% to 40% of the energy in this country is used to heat and cool our buildings—residential and commercial. This old way is expensive, dirty, and a proven danger to life. Yet it's a problem with a solution. But we must decide to apply that solution now.

This book advocates for smaller houses, which is a strong trend in this country. Smaller houses reduce wasted space that most people don't need or use. Smaller, better-built houses teach us to curb our appetite for energy and lessen our need to build, heat, cool, and maintain that extra space we don't need or even want. Building smaller, along with building houses prefabricated—in the process using less time, fewer materials, and using both more efficiently—is the sanest and wisest recipe for home construction, for now and for the future.

INTRODUCTION

SMALL HOUSES BECOME MORE POPULAR EVERY year. Besides simply being more manageable than big houses, small houses cost less to build. If constructed using smart modern design, technology, and materials, a small house is more comfortable, costs less to maintain, and uses less energy to heat and cool.

As the population of North American empty nesters grows, the number of these *downsized* houses grows too, houses that are smaller and less costly to build and maintain. Young people newly out of school and starting their professions want houses of their own but are often on a limited budget. Even established families are recognizing that they don't need so much room, but they want a smaller house with space that is versatile and can be used for all their regular needs.

Others, often city dwellers, frequently opt for weekend/vacation houses by the beach, in the woods, near a ski slope, or on a lake. Of these second homes, small houses are the most popular. They create a more intimate environment for family getaways. They require less upkeep and maintenance. There's less to clean. Some even become retirement homes for the parents when their children leave the nest.

The cost of heating and cooling is, as expected, far less for a smaller house. This book offers advice, examples, and solutions for multiple ways energy can be preserved, by constructing a more efficient envelope, with optimal solar orientation, and by using more efficient products and systems.

BUILDING BETTER NOT LARGER

As you'll see throughout this book, building *better* is preferable to building *bigger*. Varying in size from the smallest at a mere 350 sq. ft. to the largest at just over 2,000 sq. ft., these houses demonstrate how a dwelling built with smart construction techniques can provide all the room a family might need. And they show how building an energy-efficient, healthy environment beats living in a large drafty house that contains rooms that may rarely, if ever, be used. Saving on building materials for a smaller house not only saves money but also helps preserve the environment.

UNIQUE PLACES TO LIVE

The houses showcased here are found in some of the most interesting locations I have seen. The Solar Laneway House, for instance, stands where a garage once stood. Since 2009, Vancouver has seen more than 1,600 of these new homes, built to fill a need for in-city living at a reduced cost. The term *laneway* refers to the alley, or rear lane, people use to

The Little House on the Ferry was built in three sections so they could be used as needed.

Photo courtesy of Trent Bell

access garages or that rubbish collectors use to get to trash bins.

The Lake Union Floating Home allows an empty-nester couple to wake up to gorgeous views of the sea. The Westport Beach House is a lovely example of a home built in an area that is close to the ocean; where many houses are still damaged by past flooding.

All these houses were built with a conscious attempt to preserve the land on which they now stand. Little House on the Ferry was built in three parts, not only to avoid disturbing the rocky terrain by executing one small part of the overall structure at a time (rather than one large construction proj-

ect all at once) but also, once built, to require energy only for the unit/units in use. Although large for this book, the Dawnsknoll House is smaller than most of the nearby houses in Santa Monica, Calif. The homeowners wanted to preserve the outdoor space while limiting the construction footprint as much as possible. The owners of the Vashon Island House used just a small part of their land, maintaining the rest in its natural state.

ECO-FRIENDLY PREFAB BUILDING

It doesn't make sense to try to save energy but then waste materials in on-site construction. Prefab construction resolves that issue. Material used

A side view of the SU+RE House from the 2015 Solar Decathlon. The electric car was powered by excess energy produced by the house's PV panels.

Photo courtesy of Juan Alicante

in a factory is recycled and reused. Wood cutoffs from one house are used on other houses, metal is recycled and excess drywall is returned to the manufacturer. In some factories, wood is cut up and used for heating the factory. Materials are shipped in bulk, which reduces costs in addition to saving fuel. Building with prefabrication methods is a wonderful solution to minimizing waste.

For some reason, prefabrication has the persisting stigma of being plain and cookie cutter. One look at the houses in this book, however, and doubters will shed their reservations. All of these houses were custom built and are anything but plain. Each is clearly unique and special.

MULTIPLE PREFAB METHODS

A variety of prefab methods were used depending on the house style, location, available manufacturers, and needs of the homeowner.

New prefab methods are often developed even by young adults still in school. Each year I am wowed by the houses created by students in North America and around the world who participate in the Solar Decathlon sponsored by the U.S. Department of Energy. These are the architects, builders, manufacturers, and homeowners of the future. They are the ones who will influence construction in the years to come. And based on what I've seen, our future will be very bright. Every two years when the Solar Decathlon occurs in the United States, students present new and innovative methods and materials that they sometimes develop on their own.

TOP LEFT: The Lake Union Floating House on Lake Union in Washington was built using a unique hybrid construction that included some techniques used for marine construction.

Photo courtesy of Steve Keating

BOTTOM LEFT: The Westport Beach House in Connecticut was built using a panelized system after the owner's previous house was severely damaged by Hurricane Sandy.

Photo courtesy of Michael Biondo

The Solar Laneway House, built with SIPs, is one of the many laneway homes that can now potentially be built in Vancouver, Canada, thanks to a law enacted in 2009.

Photo courtesy of Colin Perry

This book features three amazing examples of Solar Decathlon innovation:
- The SU+RE House, built by a team at Stevens Institute of Technology, is designed to survive the next hurricane on the New Jersey shore.
- UrbanEden, designed and built by a group at the University of North Carolina, Charlotte, who developed a revolutionary prefabrication method using an environmentally friendly concrete.

- The DesertSol House, built by students at the University of Nevada, Las Vegas, conscious of water conservation, found ways to save water and use it for cooling.

Other houses in the book demonstrate additional interesting prefab construction methods. Several were built modular, such as the Bayview Cottage, the Sonoma Residence, the Bonsall House, the weeZero House, and the eHab Cabin. Others were

A covered walkway leads from the house to the garage of the Cousins River Residence in Freeport, Maine.

Photo courtesy of Trent Bell

panelized with a variety of unique systems, such as the Hilltop House's panelized components within a timber frame. The Dawnsknoll House was built using galvanized steel components.

Structural insulated panels (SIPs), long known to be incredibly efficient, do not disappoint here. A truly prefabulous example in the book is the John's Island House, built with earthquake-resistant panels. Several others such as the FabCab® houses—Whidbey Island House, Vashon Island House, and Sandpoint Cabin—all were built with timber frames, SIPs, petite footprints, and well-used space.

Other methods are more unusual, such as the Lake Union Floating Home, which was built like a boat on land. All parts for the Halcyon Hill House were precut and numbered in a factory, and the building was erected on site. The Lakeside Container Cottage was built using shipping containers.

All of these methods save materials, save time, and create very efficient house envelopes.

SMALL BUT NOT TINY

This book has been arranged from the smallest houses to the largest. Although the title of the book implies that the houses presented within are small, a few might be considered average size in

some communities. I included houses that are just over 2,000 sq. ft. because they are such special prefabs—beautiful, energy efficient, and environmentally friendly yet still smaller than the average new house.

It should be noted that although some of these houses are very small, they are still code compliant and attached to sewerage and water, making them more convenient to live in than the popular new tiny houses: Although not mobile, these homes are more user-friendly.

THE IDEAL HOME

The ideal home is one that is attractive, comfortable, maintains a healthy interior environment, conserves energy and water, exceeds the local building requirements, is cost-effective, requires minimal maintenance, and is constructed in as short a time as possible.

Each of the 32 houses in this book meets those criteria. They are located in a variety of climates and use a range of innovative prefabrication methods across many different styles. Each was built thoughtfully. All are small, efficient, and kind to the environment.

CASITA DE INVIERNO

Steel SIPs

PHOTOGRAPHER
Jeremy Scott (except where noted)

ARCHITECT/INTERIOR DESIGNER
David J. Bailey/
Stephanie Harrison-Bailey

GENERAL CONTRACTOR
Sebastian Design Implementation

SIPS SHELL BUILDER
Marquis Construction & Development, Inc.

MANUFACTURER
PermaTherm

CERTIFICATIONS
ENERGY STAR®
(pending)

LOCATION
Ybor City, Tampa, Fla.

SIZE
352 sq. ft.

FACING PAGE: The siding of this tiny shotgun house is local Florida cypress, the roof is zinc-coated steel Galvalume, and the fencing is long-lasting pressure-treated pine that's milled for historic accuracy. As found throughout the Gulf Coast, crushed shell is used in lieu of gravel or crushed stone for landscaping.

ARCHITECTS DAVID BAILEY & STEPHANIE HARRISON-Bailey wanted to build a Florida vacation home as a much-needed respite from the harsh New York City winters. Designing and overseeing construction of the house also gave them an opportunity to work together as a couple.

GETTING JUST THE RIGHT PROPERTY

With a background in multiunit housing, David and Stephanie originally planned to build a micro-residential development of four townhouses on their 50-ft. by 100-ft. lot. However the economic downturn that began in 2008 put things into a new perspective. Suddenly, this relatively "big" townhouse development seemed to need scaling back. It seemed more appropriate to David and Stephanie to sketch out a smaller, simpler scheme, which eventually became a small home for themselves. They already understood the unique zoning of the Tampa, Florida, neighborhood known as Ybor City from previous developments, so this seemed the right location to give it a try.

As the recession dragged on, their sketches became simpler and simpler, until the plan was distilled into three simple squares, each one roughly 10 ft. by 10 ft. Essentially, they had rediscovered the so-called shotgun shacks, the long narrow houses that had predominated Ybor City generations ago as homes for cigar factory workers.

WHY SO SMALL?

Ybor City was the perfect micro-neighborhood to experiment with a smaller size home, and the only neighborhood in Tampa that allows such small home construction. (Zoning codes in many U.S. cities don't allow houses this small, which some people think suggests a lack of affluence and may lower surrounding property values.)

The Baileys are fond of this neighborhood, which has a long history of small houses. From the beginning, cost and quality were their major concerns. By building and living small, it was feasible to have two residences. Even though they both have lived in larger homes, the Baileys are urbanites at heart and love their tiny New York City studio. "It was natural, then, that we'd design something even smaller as a vacation cottage," David says. "Throughout the whole design and construction process, it was curious to experience the number of people who tried to talk us out of building small. Now that it's built, those same people have really embraced the result!"

Walls throughout the interior are made of traditional horizontal beadboard, while the flooring is red oak. The furnishings are all sourced within 10 miles of the house. Ceilings are 15 ft. high at the ceiling ridge to make room for heat to rise away from occupants and to give the illusion of more space.

Photo courtesy of Rich Montalbano

Although their New York apartment is technically larger than the Casita, the Baileys Tampa home feels much more spacious because of the high ceilings. By adding volume in the height, the couple made the space feel larger than the actual footprint. The Baileys prioritized the space according to what they would be spending time doing while at the house. Because they would rather go out for meals than cook, they opted to make the kitchen a small space; the dining table is accessible but is opened only when they need it, and the chairs hang on the walls (see the photos on the facing page). Further to that space-saving end, the opening between the living room and the kitchen has no swinging door to take up precious space.

"On the flip side, this house is where we go to relax and escape, so we kept the living room well sized and added an eastern-facing porch so we'd have plenty of room to lounge around reading books and enjoying café con leche (Cuban-style coffee, a local favorite)," David says.

FITTING IN WITH THE NEIGHBORHOOD

Founded in the 1880s by cigar manufacturers as a community for their factory workers from Cuba, Spain, and Italy, Ybor City is an important historic district of Tampa. Keeping the house consistent with its surroundings was important to David and Stephanie and necessary for the neighborhood's architectural review board. According to David, "We wanted to stay true to the small cottages the cigar rollers lived in when Ybor was founded, so we incorporated many of the simple but beautiful details that are found on those older houses in the neighborhood—like a steeply pitched metal roof, wood siding, and interior beadboard paneling."

TOP AND BOTTOM: When folded and stored against the wall, the drop-leaf table frees valuable floor space in this narrow shotgun house. Folding chairs hang from wall hooks when not in use.

STEEL SIPS

Residential structural insulated panels (SIPs) are thick layers of rigid insulation sandwiched between two layers of structural material, such as plywood, oriented-strand board (OSB), or metal. SIPs made with metal in the form of steel panels are often used for commercial construction but sometimes, as in this house, on residential projects. For owners and builders, steel-skinned SIPs offer an exterior envelope that's 15 times more air tight than traditional construction.

Steel SIPs are lighter than traditional OSB panels and so require no crane for installation. They are also termite, mold, and rot resistant. Because Florida is often hit by hurricanes, building codes there require installation of steel hurricane straps in wood-framed construction. Steel-skinned SIPs essentially turn the entire panel into a hurricane strap, because of the strength of the metal versus wood panels. Like other SIPs, steel SIPs can be erected quickly, are very energy efficient, have low environmental impact (they use recycled material), and are very strong. The SIPs used for the Casita were from PermaTherm (permatherm.net).

HEATING AND COOLING

The space is so small and the building envelope so tight that a single mini-split system keeps the house perfectly comfortable, even in the hot Tampa summer. The unit is mounted high in the bedroom, and air is pushed from the bedroom across the loft space and into the living room. This simple loop of airflow is achieved by running the bedroom ceiling fan in reverse, to raise the cool air, then using the living room ceiling fan to pull the air down, resulting in a steady loop of conditioned air through the house. Despite its Florida location, the high ceilings, tight SIPs building envelope, and cross ventilation keep the space comfortable for much of the year without air-conditioning.

The regional plantings—including grasses, succulents, bushes, and trees—on the property are Florida friendly, requiring less water than many other varieties in this relatively dry climate.

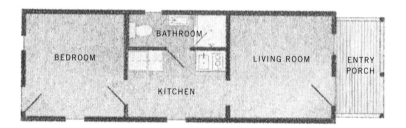

BEDROOM   BATHROOM   LIVING ROOM   ENTRY PORCH   KITCHEN

GREEN FEATURES

- Helical pier foundation system
- Recycled steel on roof and SIPs
- Locally sourced cypress siding (with natural resistance to insects and decay)
- Low-flow faucets and showers
- Low volatile organic compound (VOC) finishes
- Permeable paving
- Native plantings

ENERGY-EFFICIENT FEATURES

- Optimal solar orientation
- High-efficiency windows
- Mini-split heat pump
- Tankless water heater
- SIPs envelope
- LED lighting
- ENERGY STAR–rated appliances
- ENERGY STAR–rated ceiling fans

A POSITIVE REACTION FROM THE NEIGHBORS

Throughout construction, neighbors from Ybor and beyond stopped by to check on the progress or ask questions about the house. Many passersby couldn't believe the tiny building taking shape would be a house.

"One of our favorite things about the little house is the reaction it garners," David says. "No matter the walk of life, people are constantly smiling and becoming engaged as they pass by. It's so fulfilling to see people from ages 8 to 80 break into a big grin when they see the Casita. That's how we know the little house is a success."

HELICAL PIER FOUNDATION

Helical, or spiral, piers are manufactured steel foundation pins that are driven (or screwed) into the soil to a depth below the frost line using hydraulic machinery. For this project, eight giant screws were inserted to support the house and keep it anchored even in the event of a hurricane.

While the system is well tested and widely used in other parts of the United States and the world, the technology is rarely used in the Southeast, and then usually as a fix for sinkholes (helical piers can be screwed either into the adjacent stronger soil or into the stronger soil below the weak sinkhole pocket; they can also be driven to greater depths than traditional foundations can be dug). As a result, a significant amount of time was needed to educate suppliers, engineers, contractors, and building officials on how the design would work in this location.

The cost of installing a helical pier system is more expensive than a traditional foundation with concrete footings, but the benefits outweighed the costs for this home. Installation occurs in one day and with very little disruption to the site and surrounding property. In addition, if homeowners ever want to relocate the house all they have to do is disconnect utilities, cut the "screws," hoist the house onto the back of a flatbed trailer, and leave little evidence that the house was even there. The helical pier foundation used for this house was from L.R.E. Ground Services (lregsi.com).

The house under construction (here the rear of the house) clearly shows the helical piers that support and anchor the structure. The helicals for this little house are driven 9 ft. to 12 ft. deep; by contrast, traditional concrete piers go only 1 ft. or 2 ft. into the ground, depending on the climate.

Photo courtesy of David Bailey

EHAB CABIN

Steel Frame/Modular
Construction

PHOTOGRAPHER
Michael Cole (except
where noted)

ARCHITECT/INTERIOR
DESIGNER
E. Cobb Architects

SITE BUILDER
Johnson & Hunter

MANUFACTURER
Dogwood Industries

LOCATION
Seattle, Wash.

SIZE
450 sq. ft.

WHEN HOME CONSTRUCTION DRIED UP DURING THE economic downturn of 2008, Architect Eric Cobb decided to develop a concept he'd been thinking about for a while. Instead of reducing staff, Cobb gave one of his architects the job of helping develop a house that could be built entirely in a factory and made so strong that it would hold up under nearly any environmental extreme. Factory construction would include all systems—even those that would allow the house to function off the grid. The plan was for a 100% complete prefabricated cabin, built to withstand an extreme range of environments, including mountain snow loads, hurricane winds, seismic events, and marine environments.

The architects wanted to take full advantage of factory fabrication and its much higher construction standards and assemblies, while also gaining efficiencies in the process. The eHAB dwelling was to be effectively livable when it left the factory and, once delivered, would require minimal maintenance. The architects filed a patent application for this dwelling, believed to be the first of its kind ever conceptualized.

BUILT WITH STEEL

The house was designed without any wood structural components, making it resistant to termites and rot. All structural elements are steel, with insulated steel wall panels spanning from floor to roof and filled with uninterrupted foam insulation. All exterior steel is either galvanized or treated with Kynar® (a resin-based coating that protects against weathering and pollution) to prevent rusting. Additional batt insulation on the interior of the walls makes up a total insulation R-value of 43. (A typically framed house with 6 in. of fiberglass batting would have an R-value of 15.) Instead of drywall on the interior, the architects used plywood panels, which are very durable and offer the warmth and aesthetics of a cabin.

According to Cobb's plan, each eHAB dwelling would arrive equipped to accept a broad range of systems, specifically selected for each installation based on need dictated by location. These systems would include wind and solar energy generation, heat storage, gray water management, and a composting toilet. The goal was for the house to be viable off-grid in remote areas, with minimal or no maintenance needs for the building, though systems would still need occasional maintenance.

DESIGNING A HOUSE FOR THE EITELS

The design concept became a reality when Julie and Nick Eitel approached Eric in 2010. They wanted to build a single-family residence on top of a bluff and an office/guesthouse at the base of the bluff, which was vir-

The steel exterior and contemporary design give the house a unique appearance. On the lower level, a small room houses mechanical equipment and storage space for recreational water equipment. A path leads from the house to Lake Washington.

The living room offers beautiful views of Lake Washington through the glass facade on the south side of the house.

tually inaccessible by land. Because this office/ guesthouse would have been costly to build in conventional fashion, with only a barge to deliver building materials, Eric's model house would be the perfect solution—prefabricated and built to endure a marine environment.

The house took eight months to complete. The core unit was trucked from the factory in Sedro-Woolley, Wash., to Lake Union in Seattle. It

The open floor plan keeps everything visible and accessible. The center kitchen island and cabinet are on wheels and can be rolled out of the way when the Murphy bed (to the left) is lowered. Firewood is stored in a custom steel ring mounted on the wall.

was then loaded onto a barge and floated to its location in Lake Washington, where the unit was lifted onto site. A switchback path for pedestrian access was carved through the forested hillside, and the owners also installed a cable tram as an alternative way to get down to the cabin.

HEATING AND COOLING

Because of the proximity to the lake, there was no need for a cooling system. Natural ventilation is achieved via numerous windows and doors, while deep overhangs block the hot summer sun. A high-efficiency boiler and an in-floor radiant system provide the heat needed for the home, which is connected to the water and electric system of the house above.

DELIVERING A COMPLETED HOUSE

Appliances and even some furnishings were set in the house at the factory. While costs for this cabin were relatively high compared to some other prefab dwellings, this highly custom, high-performance dwelling was significantly less costly built in the factory than if built on land—particularly in this demanding location.

DUAL-FLUSH TOILETS

With water shortages around the country, homeowners are doing whatever they can to reduce water consumption. Because each toilet uses approximately 9,000 gal. of water per year, more-efficient toilets make sense. The U.S. Energy Policy Act requires that toilets made after 1994 use no more than 1.6 gal. per flush (GPF). California law reduces that amount to no more than 1.28 GPF for toilets sold in the state.

Dual-flush toilets, which can reduce water usage by up to 67%, are now readily available from many manufacturers in a variety of styles, colors, and prices. They look like traditional toilets, except for the flushing handles, or buttons, which let the user select the volume of water used for each flush: a short flush for liquids (which uses as little as 0.8 gal. of water) and a long flush for solids (which uses 1.6 gal. and saves up to 8,000 gal. annually). These toilets have been available in Europe for years and are mandatory in Israel, Australia, and Singapore for new or replacement toilets.

RECYCLING STEEL

Steel has been recycled for 150 years and, according to the Steel Recycling Institute, "Steel is North America's #1 recycled material. Each year, more steel is recycled in the U.S. than aluminum, paper, glass and plastic combined." The American Iron and Steel Institute boasts that "steel retains an extremely high overall recycling rate, which in 2012, stood at 88 percent." Sources of steel are plentiful, and recycled steel can be reused without degradation in performance. And it can be recycled again and again.

Steel recycling is important because it conserves raw materials and energy. Remelting scrap requires much less energy than producing iron and steel products from iron ore. Recycling also limits the burden on landfills and the accumulation of abandoned steel products in the environment. Of eHAB's 21.5-ton total weight (excluding the foundation), approximately 72% is recycled steel—used in the structure, walls, floors, decking, roofing, stair, rails, and other miscellaneous items.

FACING PAGE: Designed and built to adapt to different sites, the outside staircase is capable of a 24-in. variation in height, up and down; the concept is similar to staircases used for airport jetways.

BELOW: A recessed wooden shower grate hides the drain in the curbless shower.

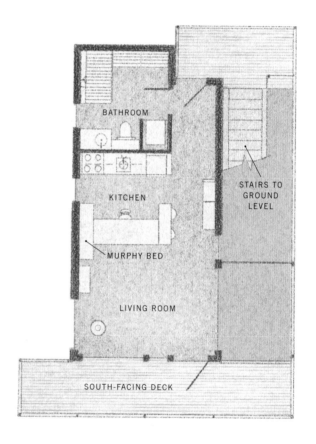

TOP: The back of the house faces a 40-ft. bluff to the north. Slats on the side of the house are for privacy and shading, while large front and rear overhangs shelter the house from hot sun in the summer but allow passive heating in the winter when the sun is lower in the sky.

BOTTOM: A full-length wooden slat screen on the cabin's east side provides privacy and weather protection while allowing light into the covered exterior stair, the south deck, and the living space.

BATHROOM

KITCHEN

STAIRS TO GROUND LEVEL

MURPHY BED

LIVING ROOM

SOUTH-FACING DECK

GREEN FEATURES
- Dual-flush toilet
- Low-flow faucets and shower
- Low-VOC finishes
- Recycled steel
- Flexible space

ENERGY-EFFICIENT FEATURES
- Triple-pane fiberglass-framed windows
- Large overhangs
- In-floor hydronic radiant heat
- Tankless water heater
- LED lighting
- ENERGY STAR–rated appliances

MODULAR CONSTRUCTION

Modules or boxes are produced in a factory under ideal conditions. Unlike site-built houses, modular houses are protected from the elements during construction, and work continues regardless of the weather. Completion of these modules depends on the requirements of the builder and homeowner. Some houses, like the eHAB Cabin, are shipped almost complete; others are left unfinished, and siding, roofing, and interior finishes are installed on site. The modules are shipped to the site on flatbed trucks or, as in this case, by barge. Once on site, a crane picks up the modules and sets them on a prepared foundation.

Modular construction offers many advantages. Modular houses are built faster and stronger (because they need to be lifted with a crane and not fall apart). And they are often built more cheaply than conventional construction. As with any factory operation, modular construction can take place 12 months a year, rain or shine. In addition, many of the materials used in building can be recycled, such as scraps of wood, metal, and drywall.

Watching a modular house being set is a wondrous thing. Arrive at the site in the morning and all you see is a foundation. Later that day or the next, as if by magic, there sits a dried-in house you can walk through. For additional information contact the Modular Building Institute (modular.org).

TOP LEFT: The modular core is lifted from a barge onto land, where the foundation waits.

BOTTOM: Once set on the foundation, the module gets its metal roof and wood screen. These items were shipped with the module but installed on site, because they would have exceeded the 16 ft. maximum width permitted for truck transport.

Photos courtesy of E. Cobb Architects

COCOON STUDIO

Modular/ Steel Frame

PHOTOGRAPHER
Genevieve Garruppo
(except where noted)

ARCHITECT
Lisa R. E. Zaloga,
Architects

PREFAB DESIGN AND
BUILD
Cocoon9

GENERAL CONTRACTOR
Owen & Broniecki
Construction

INTERIOR DESIGNER
Sarah Storms

LOCATION
Southampton, N.Y.

SIZE
480 sq. ft.

CHRIS BURCH HAS A LOVE OF DESIGN AND A passion for giving people what they want. By paying close attention to the tiny home movement and the allure of space efficiency, he created a premium version of a small, prefabricated home that has quality production, high-end finishes, and energy-conscious features.

His vision was that of a factory-built house with a resort-like environment. It would be light and airy and would welcome in the outdoors through 9-ft. floor-to ceiling windows. As an entrepreneur in many fields, Chris knew he needed the right partner. He approached his long-time friend and contractor Ed Mahoney, head of his 90-year-old family business, EB Mahoney Builders, for expertise to help create his home design and build firm, Cocoon9.

VISIONS OF EFFICIENCY

Once he'd nailed down his design vision, Chris set out to reduce the time it takes to construct a custom home (often more than a year) and by building prefab to eliminate the on-site delays of site-built houses due to weather and material delivery issues. The company's "Cocoons" are manufactured in a factory to make use of precision engineering and speed. They can be delivered to the site, fully assembled, in a remarkable four months. According to Chris, "The idea of a plug-and-play home fueled our vision."

Emphasis is on high-quality, space-efficient design and construction and on the use of both passive and active energy efficiencies. Passive heating and cooling are carried out through cross ventilation and large windows. The active energy comes from a highly efficient mini-split system. The company uses Forest Stewardship Council® (FSC) approved certified wood, LED lighting, and well-insulated walls and windows that maintain a constant home temperature. Space-saving features, such as casework to fold and hide away beds, and flexible-use rooms ensure that this high-tech home is easy to operate.

The use of steel framing creates a very strong structure. The company's homes can withstand hurricane winds of 150 miles per hour. Because some of their houses are shipped internationally from China, they wanted the houses to be strong enough to endure a trip across the ocean. Steel construction also allows the company to build houses that easily support floor-to-ceiling windows and wide-open spaces.

The siding of this 480-sq.-ft. rectangular building is recyclable HDPE wood plastic composite. The decking is FSC-certified bamboo.

Photo courtesy of Cocoon9

ETHANOL FIREPLACES

Ethanol fireplaces are flueless and ventless so they can be located anywhere inside or outside the house and can even be moved from one location to another. Instead of emitting dangerous fumes, they emit steam vapor and carbon dioxide. There is no toxic smoke.

These fireplaces burn clean and create no soot or ashes, require no gas lines, and are easy to install. Tabletop models put out 2,000 BTUs to 3,000 BTUs, freestanding models 4,000 BTUs to 8,000 BTUS, and built-in models 6,000 BTUs to 28,000 BTUS (depending on the unit). And none of that heat escapes up the chimney.

Ethanol fireplaces are environmentally friendly because, unlike standard fireplaces, they reduce energy loss from the house. Also, the ethanol is made from renewable sources such as corn, potatoes, and rice. Operating costs remain low at about $2 per hour, depending on the unit. Ceramic stones and logs can be added to make the fireplace look more like a wood burner. The only thing missing is the pleasant scent of a wood-burning fireplace. The ethanol fireplace in this house is from Ignis (ignisproducts.com).

TOP: During the day, the Murphy bed folds up into the white-lacquered cabinetry, freeing the space for other uses. The lighting is all LED.

BOTTOM: The kitchenette features compact appliances such as an induction stovetop and undercounter refrigerator.

Photo courtesy of Cocoon9

Full-height floor-to-ceiling sliding windows open the living room to the outdoors—it's almost like having a removable exterior wall. The white rectangle on the back wall is a swiveling television that can be viewed from either the living room or the bedroom beyond. The see-through ethanol fireplace below the television helps warm the house on the coldest days. Flooring throughout the house is recyclable laminate vinyl.

THE PRODUCTION PROCESS

Cocoon houses sold domestically are built in New Jersey, whereas international orders are fulfilled in China. A Cocoon house is delivered on a flatbed truck and placed on a preset foundation. Utilities are connected in less than a week.

Cocoon's sale price includes all finishes, fixtures, components (such as in-wall wiring, plumbing, and HVAC lines), and equipment (such as the water heater, garbage disposal, and heat pump). The homeowner is responsible for permits, the foundation, and utility hook-ups as well as the cost of installation and transportation, which vary depending on the destination.

A company based in China that uses FSC-certified wood makes the high-density polyethylene (HDPE) wood plastic composite siding for the houses. The material is formed from wood fiber and recyclable plastic. It feels and looks like wood and is low maintenance.

The company envisions their homes as primary residences, vacation homes, guest cottages, personal office spaces, pool houses, and even boathouses. Chris reports that the Cocoon units offer "a different approach to sustainable luxury, appealing to those who value sophisticated design details and premium features. Our customer also appreciates a sleek, intimate footprint that still feels comfortable, versatile, and spacious."

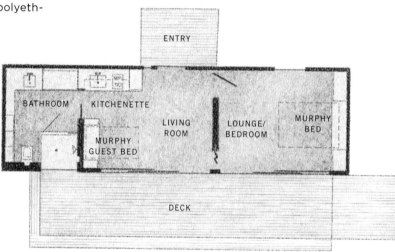

GREEN FEATURES
- Small footprint
- Recyclable HDPE wood plastic composite siding
- Recyclable laminate vinyl flooring
- FSC-certified bamboo decking
- Dual-flush toilets
- Low-flow faucets and showers
- Low- or no-VOC finishes

ENERGY-EFFICIENT FEATURES
- PV panels
- High-efficiency windows
- Thermally broken, low-E, argon-insulated glazing
- Mini-split system
- Tankless water heater
- Continuous polyurethane spray-foam insulation
- LED lighting
- ENERGY STAR–rated appliances
- Ethanol fireplace

For privacy, smart glass technology transforms the shower window from clear to opaque.

Photo courtesy of Cocoon9

THE SPACE-SAVING MAGIC OF THE WALL-HUNG TOILET

With its tank hidden away inside the wall, a wall-hung toilet adds up to 12 in. of floor space, which makes it especially practical in small bathrooms. It uses about 20% less water than standard toilets and is more hygienic: Because the toilet doesn't rest on the floor (the drain is inside the wall), it's easier to clean beneath it. For maintenance, the wall panel opens to access the workings.

The concept was introduced in Europe in the 1980s, but its popularity here has vastly increased, particularly because of the current emphasis on smaller spaces and the increased interest in modern design. (These toilets also look excellent in more traditional houses.) The three parts of the toilet are the tank (or *in-wall carrier*), the bowl/seat, and the flush panel (which comes in many styles). For the Cocoon Studio, the parts were manufactured by different companies and bought separately, which is the case with many of these types of toilets.

Mounting a wall-hung toilet is obviously easier in new construction before drywall goes up. Retrofitting one of these fixtures requires that the wall and the floor be opened to accommodate the in-wall tank and drain. The tank also requires the wall be built with 2×6 studs. (More often than not, interior walls are built with 2×4s, even in bathrooms.)

For more information on the in-wall carrier in this house, see the Geberit® website (geberit-northamerica.com). For information about the wall-hung toilet, see Roca's website (roca.com).

SANDPOINT CABIN

Timber Frame/SIPs

ARCHITECT
FabCab

BUILDER
Selle Valley Construction

LOCATION
Sagle, Idaho

SIZE
550 sq. ft.

THE SANDPOINT CABIN IN NORTHERN IDAHO IS A vacation home for Suzanne, Greg, and their two sons. They travel here frequently from their primary residence in Seattle to enjoy the beautiful scenery, hiking trails, fishing, mountain biking, and lush greenery.

A CHALLENGING SITE

Though the land has beautiful views, it was not without some challenges when it came to building the cabin. The steep slope contributed to the trials of construction at this location, requiring large posts in concrete footings for the foundation. A storage and mechanical closet room is located under the deck, enclosed by horizontal cedar boards that also hide the posts from view. In time, the natural landscape will help minimize the visual height of this wall as the plants mature. The deck is five steps down from the cabin to preserve the line of sight from the interior to the lakeshore below.

QUALITY OVER QUANTITY

The goal in designing and building this house was to create a very cozy home with a small footprint and an emphasis on quality over quantity. Although the house is small, it feels spacious, largely due to the high ceilings and the absence of an upper wall between the bedroom and living room. Being able to see the ceiling continue above, across, and between rooms makes the space feel larger (see the photo on p. 32). The wide barn-door opening between the bedroom and living room also contributes to the sense of spaciousness (see "Sliding Barn Doors" on p. 34).

Items in the house were sized to allow as much space as possible. In the kitchen, a narrow and spatially efficient refrigerator/freezer makes extra room for other necessary features, including lots of storage cabinets and a dishwasher. An efficient two-burner induction cooktop is located under a convection/microwave oven combo with a built-in exhaust vent.

The wall of windows on the west-southwest side not only brings in a good deal of light but also helps this small cabin feel larger than it is. A covered deck at the entry leads down to an open deck to the west, extending the living space in good weather.

BUILDING WITH TIMBER FRAME AND SIPS

The owners chose a timber frame for the beauty of its construction, which is apparent in the interior as well as exterior of the house. As a bonus, the strong timber frame allows for wide-open spaces rather than an interior with many supporting walls as is required with typical construction.

The cabin is set on the side of a steep slope, allowing unobstructed views of Lake Pend Oreille.

Photo by Rob Yagid for *Fine Homebuilding*, ©The Taunton Press, Inc.

TIMBER FRAME/ POST AND BEAM

Traditional timber frames are created with mortise-and-tenon joinery and secured with wood pegs. Carefully measured, cut, and joined, they create a strong, tight frame for homes, barns, or other structures.

For houses and other large structures, timber frames are built using heavy timbers rather than the dimensional wood (such as 2×4s) used for traditional framing. Post-and-beam frames are similar but can include exposed metal fasteners (commonly black hardware) and may include engineered wood.

Timber frames have been constructed for hundreds of years—in earlier times built using axes, chisels, and other hand tools. Today, most frames are prefabricated in a factory using sophisticated machinery; the parts are numbered and put together on site. Frames are sometimes hidden behind finished walls but are often kept visible in the interior of the house to show off the craftsmanship and to provide an interesting, warm design feature. Timber frames are capable of bearing heavy weight and so do not require as many vertical support posts and bearing walls as used in traditional construction. This creates a much more flexible floor plan. At the end of the life cycle of the home, these posts and beams can also be reused for other purposes.

A cozy couch sits next to a wall of windows that frames a dramatic view of the lake. High ceilings and open areas above the walls on either side make the space feel bigger than it is. The ceiling is continuous among the different areas of the cabin, further increasing the sense of spaciousness.

Photo courtesy of Marie-Dominique Verdier

The kitchen is appropriately compact yet provides plenty of storage. At one end of the counter, a 24-in. refrigerator takes up minimal space, a nice feature for such a small footprint. At the other end, a two-burner induction cooktop is more thermally efficient than either gas or electric models. For cross ventilation, a window above the sink brings in natural light and air.

Photo courtesy of Marie-Dominique Verdier

SLIDING BARN DOORS

Barn doors serve as unique elements inside a house, not only for their functionality but also as decorative design elements. They can be a space saver, performing the duties of an ordinary door while staying flush with the wall—which makes them perfect for use in rooms where there is no space for doors to swing in and out. Barn doors can be used to close off rooms, hide television sets, or divide a room; they can also be used as closet doors or as exterior doors. A multitude of designs are available to fit any type of decor from rustic to modern.

Barn doors can be bought as antiques, salvaged from old barns or houses, built by handy do-it-yourselfers, or purchased new. Sometimes authentic old barn doors are restored or old doors from other houses are repurposed as barn doors. These can be used in pairs or individually; hung from a bar with rollers or coasters at the top or a rail at the bottom. The barn door hardware in the Sandpoint Cabin was supplied by Real Sliding Hardware (realslidinghardware.com).

FACING PAGE: A luxurious bathroom provides spa-like comfort, which is impressive for a cabin with such a small footprint. Features include a barrier-free shower, a large vanity, and a stacked washer and dryer. The cabinets are Douglas fir, which matches the timber frame.

BELOW: Double barn doors create a large opening between the bedroom and living space, which makes the cabin feel bigger and less compartmentalized. Depending on the needs of the occasion, the doors can be closed or open to give the space flexibility of use.

Photos courtesy of Marie-Dominique Verdier

Suzanne and Greg opted to build using SIPs because they wanted the home to be energy efficient, fast to build, and have minimal construction waste on site. The SIPs have a higher R-value (see the Glossary on p. 222) than typical insulated stick-frame construction. In addition, there is no thermal transfer between the inside and the outside because no wall studs interrupt the insulation layer. As a result, the insulation not only has a higher R-value than a conventionally framed building but is also continuous, with panels tightly fitted into each other.

Principal architect Emory Baldwin of FabCab says, "The owners love their cabin so much that they want to build another one. They might end up having two or three FabCab structures on their property so that they can have more guests visit/stay. They have even talked about having a small FabCab compound in the future."

Broad expanses of glass admit a lot of natural light into the cabin. This creates a direct line of sight to the porch and deck outside and the view beyond. A recess for a bench makes the most of the corner space just inside the entry.

Photo by Rob Yagid for *Fine Homebuilding*, ©The Taunton Press, Inc.

KITCHEN

BATHROOM

BEDROOM

ENTRY PORCH

LIVING ROOM

DECK

GREEN FEATURES
- Small footprint
- Flexible spaces
- Recycled metal roof
- FSC-certified flooring
- No carpeting
- GREENGUARD™-certified quartz counters with recycled content
- Cabinetry with FSC-certified no added urea formaldehyde (NAUF) plywood
- Dual-flush toilet
- Zero-VOC paint
- Locally sourced materials as available
- Dedicated recycling station
- Drought-tolerant, native plantings

ENERGY-EFFICIENT FEATURES
- Passive solar orientation
- High-efficiency windows with tinting
- Daylighting
- Deep roof overhangs
- Natural cross ventilation
- Ductless mini-split heat pump
- Tankless water heater
- Air sealing
- SIPs
- LED and CFL lighting
- ENERGY STAR–rated appliances
- Induction cooktop
- Prewired for PV and solar hot water panels

The covered entry porch and deck add lots of outdoor living space to this small house.

INDUCTION COOKING

Induction cooktops contain copper coils beneath the cooking surface that receive an electric current, producing a magnetic field that induces current through ferrous (magnetic) pots. This latter current heats the pots—the cooktop, however, remains relatively cool.

These cooktops are more energy efficient, heat faster, and are more consistent than traditional electric ranges and are as instantaneous as gas burners. With induction cooking, energy is supplied directly to the cooking vessel by the magnetic field, and almost all of the source energy is transferred to that vessel. With gas and traditional electric stoves, a good deal of the energy dissipates into the air and surrounding surfaces.

Induction cookers are easy to clean because the cooking surface is flat and smooth and does not get hot enough to make spilled food burn and stick. The burner shuts down automatically when iron or steel cookware is removed. This also means induction cooktops are safer than conventional units because there's no risk of burning little fingers. These appliances require no gas lines; and a ductless hood eliminates the need for another opening in the exterior of the house.

One of the drawbacks to induction cooking is that the pots must be compatible with the stovetop, which means you can only use pots made of magnetic materials. Another drawback is that the glass ceramic surface can be marred by a significant impact or scratched by sliding pots. Furthermore, aluminum foil can melt onto the surface, permanently damaging the cooktop. The induction stove used in this house is a two-burner model supplied by Fagor® (fagoramerica.com).

LAKESIDE
CONTAINER COTTAGE

Shipping Containers

PHOTOGRAPHER
Kevin Walsh
Photography

ARCHITECT
Christopher Bittner
obrARCHITECTURE

LOCATION
San Diego County, Calif.

SIZE
720 sq. ft.

HOMEOWNERS SHAWN AND MICHAEL MCCONKEY had dreamed of building a container house for years. Michael is an architectural engineer and construction superintendent for a large commercial general contractor and was acquainted with architect Christopher Bittner through their past work together. For the Lakeside Container Cottage, they collaborated on design, and Michael oversaw construction.

Michael did about two-thirds of the work himself and, with the help of a general contractor, completed the house over a two-year period. Meanwhile Michael and Shawn lived on site in their recreational vehicle. They now use the Lakeside Container Cottage as their main residence but plan to turn it into a guesthouse when they build a larger container house for themselves on their 6-acre property.

BUILDING WITH CONTAINERS

Michael and Christopher first worked together building a farm stand out of shipping containers for Suzie's Farm in San Diego. The lessons they learned on that project came in handy when building the Lakeside Cottage.

The seemingly indestructible containers lose much of their rigidity when the sides are modified, as when cutting openings for windows and doors. To compensate for this loss of strength, Michael and Christopher devised structural reinforcements that didn't change the look of the container or lower its inside height. They also learned to be very conscience about waterproofing the container with flashing and welding.

THE CHALLENGES OF WORKING WITH NEW MATERIALS

Christopher and Michael spent a lot of time getting permits and approvals because the county building department was unfamiliar with this type of construction. Ultimately, it took six months to get the building permit. Special inspections for welding, concrete, masonry, and soils were required during construction—more inspections than are generally required for conventional home construction. "Anyone wanting to pursue this type of construction should thoroughly interview builders to be sure they are up to the task," Christopher points out.

Another challenge was joining conventional building materials to the containers. Compared to standard house construction, it is more difficult to attach dissimilar materials to steel than it is to wood. Because the house is in a seismically active zone, the connection was even more challenging. To make the containers watertight, sheet-metal flashing had to be welded on. And the flashing had to be both strong and flexible because the steel containers expand and contract more than a wood structure.

Located in a wildfire zone, the house has an exterior that's completely noncombustible (with dual pane-tempered exterior glass, Class A roofing materials, and fire sprinklers). Siding and soffit panels are cement board and the roofing is single-ply TPO.

GETTING THE INSULATION RIGHT

To build walls inside the containers, Michael installed drywall over metal studs. Wood furring strips create a 1-in. gap between the container and the metal studs to prevent thermal transmission of heat or cold. Closed-cell polyurethane foam sprayed in the void behind the drywall achieved an R-14 rating. The foam insulation provides an R-7 thermal rating per inch and acts as a moisture and air barrier to prevent condensation in the wall cavity. Spray foam was also used in the crawl space to get an R-19 rating in the floor. A combination of tapered and fiberglass batts was used on the roof to achieve an R-30 rating. Finally, polyurethane was sprayed around window openings to seal possible leaks.

BUILDING IN AN ENVIRONMENTALLY FRIENDLY WAY

It was important to the McConkeys that the house be as environmentally friendly as possible. Besides building with recycled shipping containers, Shawn and Michael incorporated a variety of other recycled materials into the house, such as the doorframes and laminate flooring.

The house has solar hot water panels mounted on the roof, the insulation was systematically planned and installed, and windows were placed for maximum efficiency—all to limit the use of fossil fuels. Solar panels provide the hot water to heat the hydronic radiant system, which is backed up by mini-split heat pumps for additional heating and cooling when needed.

To make the house feel roomier than its petite floor plan, Shawn and Michael raised the center ceiling of the house to 13 ft. and added a windowed garage door that opens up the living space to the outside deck.

"Building with containers is a great way to reuse materials that would otherwise sit and rot in our ports," Christopher said. "Additionally, I think people have a certain attraction to modular construction. It fascinates . . . probably for the same reasons people are fascinated by Lego®."

TOP: The stained-concrete flooring contains hydronic radiant floor heating powered by the solar panels. The concrete floors also provide thermal mass (the ability to absorb and store heat or coolness), which helps keep the house warm in winter and cool in summer.

BOTTOM: The garage door that opens up the dining area is a standard unit made for low-overhead installations, and is fitted with glass panels. Because of southern California's temperate climate, the door can stay open most of the year for ventilation. Glass panels in the door allow the light from the overhead fixture to shine through when the door is open.

The house has an open floor plan but the various areas are delineated by a change in flooring material, sliding doors, and placement of furnishings. The flooring in the kitchen is recycled laminate, while the main living areas are concrete and the bedroom has carpet squares.

SHIPPING CONTAINERS FOR LIVING

Imported goods far exceed exported goods in the United States, which results in a plentiful supply of used shipping containers. Because the containers are so inexpensive, it is often more cost-effective for companies to buy new ones than to ship back the used ones. Thus many old containers are simply discarded.

One good use for old shipping containers is to incorporate them into building construction. Containers offer several advantages. They are designed to carry heavy loads in harsh environments, are stackable, can be interlocked, and are made in several standard sizes. Properly secured, a container is capable of withstanding category 5 hurricanes, which makes them stronger than many

other structures. They can be easily transported by sea, truck, or rail and are relatively inexpensive. Used containers, which are available in a range of conditions, may cost as little as $1,500; new ones cost up to $6,000, depending on the type and where they are being sold.

Insulating a container may be a costly challenge. Most are made of Cor-Ten® steel (see p. 127), so they won't rust, but they do need to be sealed and insulated. Making attachments and alterations requires skill in metalworking (the tradesmen on this house were certified and highly skilled). Building permits for shipping container houses may also be a problem, as they were in this location.

THERMOPLASTIC POLYOLEFIN ROOFING

Thermoplastic polyolefin (TPO) single-ply roofing is finding growing favor in the residential market, although it's been available for more than 20 years commercially. This roofing membrane is more environmentally friendly than some conventional roofing materials because it can be reprocessed and recycled. The material is highly reflective, resulting in cool rooftop temperatures that lower loads on air-conditioning systems, an energy-saving feature especially valuable in warm climates. The membrane also provides exceptional resistance to ultraviolet, ozone, and chemical exposure, all of which damage conventional roofing.

TPO membrane is reinforced with a polyester fabric that provides excellent strength against breaking, tearing, and puncturing. Roofing assemblies that include TPO membranes typically have achieved UL® Class A fire ratings (the most stringent fire classification). The TPO roofing in this house was supplied by Carlisle® SynTec Systems (carlislesyntec.com).

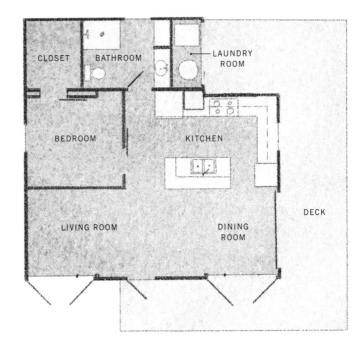

GREEN FEATURES
• Recycled containers
• Cool roof
• Low-flow faucets and showers
• Dual-flush toilet
• Recycled materials

ENERGY-EFFICIENT FEATURES
• Solar hot water panels
• Solar light tubes
• High-efficiency windows
• Large overhangs
• Energy-recovery ventilation (ERV)
• Mini-split heat pumps
• Radiant floor heating
• Tankless water heater
• CFL and LED lighting; automated timers
• ENERGY STAR–rated appliances

The deck cantilevers over the edge of the canyon, providing a view of Iron Mountain in the distance. The large overhangs block the sun in the warmer months but allow the sun to passively heat the house in the winter when the sun is lower in the sky. The container doors were retained to serve as shutters for the windows.

DESERTSOL HOUSE

Kit House

DESIGNER/BUILDER
University of Nevada,
Las Vegas students and
faculty

MANUFACTURER
PKMM Inc.

LOCATION
Solar Decathlon 2013,
Irvine, Calif.; Springs
Preserve, Las Vegas,
Nev.

SIZE
754 sq. ft.

THE DESERTSOL HOUSE, PRESENTED AT THE 2013 Solar Decathlon, was designed as a vacation/second home for seniors, retirees, young couples, or empty nesters. These are the emergent markets that are transforming the landscape of the Nevada housing market.

Eric Weber, assistant professor at the University of Nevada, Las Vegas (UNLV) School of Architecture, says that he was "particularly pleased when we won the Market Appeal competition, as this effectively demonstrated that our team addressed the needs of our target market." The team wanted to create a desert experience that would allow the inhabitants to interact with their environment while "incorporating high-tech features into the everyday comfort of living."

BUILT OFF SITE

The steel frame that supports the house was fabricated off site by a local company, and the wood framing parts were sized and precut by Red-Built™, which made a detailed, piece-by-piece analysis of the design and then shipped the exact amount of parts needed for construction, such as laminated veneer lumber (LVL) and precut engineered joists (see p. 49). Most of the parts look traditional at first glance, but studs, headers, and sill plates are all in fact engineered rather than solid wood.

The framing assembly was similar to standard construction, but with a roughly 80% reduction in waste because each piece was precut to size and marked with its specific location within the frame. Advanced framing techniques allow for wider spacing between studs and a reduction in the redundancy inherent in standard stud framing techniques—for example, the double vertical studs on each side of window openings. Advanced framing uses single studs and beam clips, which secure the vertical studs to the horizontal head and sill studs. Reducing the number of studs saves money and improves thermal efficiency.

Steel assemblies like the screens, railings, planter boxes, window projection boxes, and other assemblies, as well as the wood cabinetry, were also fabricated off site by local companies.

MATERIALS SELECTION

The design team chose materials that could both withstand the intense sunlight and exceptional dryness of this harsh environment and also echo the history of the Old West silver mining towns that dot the Nevada desert. They chose natural, durable materials—mainly wood and steel—that would age well in the desert. (Synthetic materials and coatings would not hold up in the intense heat.)

The front of the house has a deep overhang that protects the folding glass wall from the sun in the warmest months. The exterior siding is reclaimed wood siding.

Photo courtesy of Kevin Duffy

The wall that houses the media center doubles as a large storage area. The mini-split heat pump above the storage wall provides cool air when needed.

Photo courtesy of Jason Flakes

CONSERVING A VITAL RESOURCE

One of the key themes in designing and constructing the DesertSol House was how best to preserve the most valuable resource in the desert: water. To this end, the team designed a shallow pool for water between the two modules, below the narrow entranceway (see the top photo on p. 50).

Water bubbles to the surface between the stones by way of a recirculating pump, forming a desert spring. (The pump is necessary to keep mosquitos away.) The pool is designed to be a catch basin for occasional desert downpours, collecting the precious 4 in. of precipitation each year and piping it to a nearby cistern in the crawl space. The storm runoff from both roof surfaces travels through gutters to the foyer roof and then pours like a waterfall into the pond below. The water trickles over the edge of the pool and is captured in a small trough at the entry court, creating the essential sound that provides psychological comfort in this dry land.

The pool causes evaporative cooling and passes cooled, rehumidified air through a low window in the kitchen into the living spaces. The rainwater also is used in landscape irrigation, although little water is required to supply the native plants that were incorporated into the design. In time, as the plants establish roots in the surrounding soil, this desert foliage will thrive solely on the water provided by this resource.

CREATING SHADE IN THE DESERT

Careful orientation of the house, shading, and sun control are particularly important in the harsh climate of the Mojave Desert where this house was designed to be located.

The house is oriented to minimize sun exposure on the east and west walls. All glass faces north and south. The house is shaded in the warmer months by overhangs that prevent unwanted heat gain, while allowing direct sun to heat up the space in the cooler seasons. Overhangs created by the PV array along with the perforated metal shades block the sun from the glass doors while allowing hot air to escape through small openings, preventing heat buildup adjacent to windows and doors. Sliding screens can enclose the entire private deck in shade but can also be fully opened to let in the heat of the winter sun. The main building envelope is shaded by the rainscreen construction, which is reclaimed wood siding attached a few inches off the surface of the main structure to create a shaded, ventilated air gap around the building envelope. This gap prevents heat from being conducted through the wall into the house.

A "shadescreen" system also was created to add to the interior comfort of the home. Metal shades made from perforated metal and solar panels let heat pass through gaps in the covering and allow roof surfaces to shed heat rapidly.

The common areas of the house—the kitchen and living room—are on the east side. The narrow clerestory windows along the top of the north wall open to allow hot air to escape, while the ENERGY STAR–rated fan helps the room feel cooler. Reclaimed shipping crates were dismantled and repurposed into polished tongue-and-groove flooring.

Photo courtesy of Kevin Duffy

SOLAR DECATHLON

Since the first event in 2002, the Solar Decathlon has been held every two years in the United States, initially in Washington, D.C. and more recently in Irvine, Calif. Events have also been held in Spain, China, and Colombia. Thousands of students from colleges around the world design and create houses that are efficient at both collecting and converting sunlight into usable energy to compete in the event. The U.S. Department of Energy sponsors the Solar Decathlon, which is organized by the National Renewable Energy Laboratory.

Visitors tour the prefabricated houses, where student guides describe the mechanics, systems, and materials, and explain why they chose those options. The 10 contests within the competition are architecture, market appeal, engineering, communications, comfort, hot water, appliances, home entertainment, and energy balance. In 2013, affordability was added to address global economic struggles but also because many people today consider affordability a major priority in construction. For further information, visit the Solar Decathlon's website (solardecathlon.gov).

ABOVE & FACING PAGE TOP LEFT: A large sliding wall closes off the bedroom from the rest of the house. The room opens up to an outdoor screened-in area on the south side.

Photos courtesy of Kevin Duffy

FACING PAGE TOP RIGHT: The shower is curbless with the floor sloped toward the drain. The bathroom tile is porcelain.

Photo courtesy of Jason Flakes

FACING PAGE BOTTOM LEFT: A bridge between the sleeping and social areas contains the entranceway and a small sitting area. This area overlooks a small pond, which functions as a rainwater catchment basin.

Photo courtesy of Jason Flakes

LAMINATED VENEER LUMBER AND ENGINEERED JOISTS

Engineered wood products are made of multiple layers of thin wood put together with adhesives. They include laminated veneer lumber (LVL), which is produced in factories under controlled conditions and is stronger, straighter, and more uniform and stable than traditional lumber. LVL is also less likely to warp, shrink, split, or twist.

The same companies that produce LVL also manufacture I-joists, or engineered wood joists. These building parts serve as horizontal supports that run atop foundations, walls, or beams to support a ceiling or floor above. I-joists have great strength in relation to their size and weight and can carry heavy loads using less lumber than solid wood joists. Like LVL components, they resist shrinking, splitting, and twisting, which can lead to squeaky floors. I-joists are lightweight and come in long lengths, making them faster and easier to install than traditional joists while also saving both time and money.

LEFT: The catch basin, where rainwater is collected, is located behind the entry. Photo courtesy of Eric Weber/UNLV Design Build

BELOW: The solar thermal array was located to the side of the house; if placed on the roof, the panels would get too hot in the desert sun. Photo courtesy of Jason Flakes

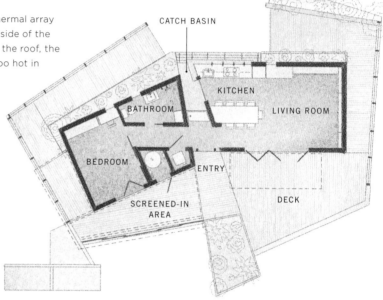

GREEN FEATURES

- Small footprint
- Flexible spaces
- Cool metal roofing (see the facing page)
- Rainscreen
- Shadescreen
- Reclaimed pallet wood for flooring
- Linoleum flooring
- Reclaimed wood for exterior wall
- Dual-flush toilet
- Low-flow faucet and showerhead
- Zero-VOC paint and adhesives
- Gray water and rainwater collection (for irrigation)
- Preconsumer cotton denim recycled material (acoustic insulation)
- Reclaimed wood for dining table

ENERGY-EFFICIENT FEATURES

- Passive solar orientation
- Solar panels
- PV panels
- High-efficiency windows
- Operable windows, optimized for passive ventilation
- Window locations selected to maximize daylighting
- Clerestory windows
- Perforated deep overhangs
- ERV
- Solar thermal heating system and hot water
- Ductless mini-split air-conditioning system
- Advanced framing
- Spray-foam insulation
- Rigid polyisocyanurate insulation
- LED lighting
- ENERGY STAR–rated appliances
- ENERGY STAR–rated ceiling fan

CREATING AN EFFICIENT BUILDING ENVELOPE

The building envelope is designed to be ultra-insulated and airtight. The advanced framing techniques, with wall studs set farther apart than in traditional construction, allow for more insulation. Wall, ceiling, and floor cavities are filled with sprayed foam insulation; 1 in. of closed-cell foam was used for its air-sealing quality and high R-value and the rest of the cavities are filled with less-expensive open-cell foam. The walls and roof structure are covered with an additional layer of foil-faced polyisocyanurate to avoid thermal bridging through the wood studs and to create a continuous layer of insulation and a radiant barrier. Rigid insulation fills voids inside all structural headers (structural members in light-frame construction that run perpendicular to the floor and ceiling joists).

Windows are tall and high to allow ample daylight to pour into living spaces, minimizing the use of electrical lighting. The windows also promote cross ventilation and cooling inside the home without the need for air-conditioning. The sloped ceilings, combined with high-mounted operable clerestory windows, help ventilate the hot air as it rises, leaving the living spaces below relatively cooler.

SOLAR DECATHLON AND BEYOND

The house came in second overall at the 2013 Solar Decathlon, taking a first place in market appeal, a second in the communications contest, and a third in engineering. DesertSol is now located at the Las Vegas Springs Preserve, a cultural historic site.

"The facility is a laboratory for best practices for building methods, energy and water use, and recycling," according to Eric Weber. "One of its primary missions is to serve as an educational tool for the community. In partnering with the Springs Preserve, Team Las Vegas hoped to locate the house within the property as a model residential building for exhibit and education. DesertSol was placed at the Springs Preserve in February 2014 and is now open to the public. UNLV personnel continue to monitor its performance, and the house will continue to serve its core function as a tool for assisting the public in creating a more sustainable future."

COOL METAL ROOFING

Cool metal roofing reflects the sun and has what engineers call *high emissivity*, which means it quickly radiates out absorbed heat. This works in any climate but is particularly suited for houses such as the DesertSol House, which is designed to be built in the desert. Cool metal roofs are available in unpainted metal, which reflects much of the solar radiation that would otherwise be absorbed into the home by materials such as asphalt roofing.

In warmer climates, prepainted or granular-coated metal roofing systems are more effective because they reflect solar energy and also cool the home by reemitting most of what solar radiation is absorbed. In locations where the bulk of the annual energy costs are for cooling, a highly reflective and highly emissive painted or granular-coated metal roof is optimal for reducing energy consumption. According to the Metal Roofing Alliance®, these painted or coated roofs actually reemit up to 90% of absorbed solar radiation. Some cool metal roofing materials are ENERGY STAR qualified. For additional information, visit the Cool Metal Roofing website (coolmetalroofing.org).

URBAN EDEN

Precast Insulated
Concrete Panels/Modular
Core

PHOTOGRAPHER
Jason Flakes (except
where noted)

ARCHITECT/BUILDER
University of North
Carolina, Charlotte Team

MANUFACTURER OF
CONCRETE PANELS
Metromont

LOCATION
Solar Decathlon 2013,
Irvine, Calif.

SIZE
800 sq. ft.

STUDENTS AT THE UNIVERSITY OF NORTH CAROLINA, Charlotte built the UrbanEden house for the 2013 Solar Decathlon competition, which was held in Irvine, Calif. They envisioned it as a house for empty nesters living in an urban area, with a strong connection between interior and exterior living spaces.

According to the team, "Our systems and strategies maintain interior comfort and healthfulness, provide adequate light for the home's interior and exterior spaces, and ensure a dependable supply of hot water, while minimizing energy consumption and maximizing power generation."

INNOVATIVE BUILDING TECHNIQUES

The students incorporated innovative building techniques into the design and construction of the house. The primary building material is a prefabricated geopolymer cement concrete panel system, which is environmentally friendly and thermally efficient (see p. 54). The post-and-beam frame is made of recycled steel and prefabricated in North Carolina.

Other innovations include an active/passive hybrid cooling system integrated into the walls of the house (see "Interactive Energy Management" on p. 57), PV panels on adjustable racks, and responsive technology that allows the house and the people in it to adapt to changing environmental conditions.

INSIDE/OUTSIDE LIVING

A glass wall with several doors divides the south-facing interior and exterior areas of the house. The combination of open outdoor space with the glass divide makes the house feel much larger than it is. Materials such as thermally modified ash flooring and laminated bamboo paneling flow between the two areas, visually tying the two together. The charming vertical garden creates privacy between the house and the surrounding urban area.

USING SOLAR ENERGY

To take best advantage of solar energy, the home is long and narrow with the longest side facing south. The wall of plants and the PV panels, which are adjustable, shade the high-performance glass on that side of the house from the high summer sun. The sun's heat and light come through in the colder months, effectively using the solar energy to heat the house.

The superior airtight windows and doors, including the south-facing glass wall, have high-performance frames made with "warm-edge" spacers (insulated areas around the glass that create barriers to heat loss),

The house frame is made from prefabricated post-and-beam steel components and precast cement panels.
Photo courtesy of UNC Charlotte

PRECAST GEOPOLYMER CEMENT CONCRETE

Students at the University of North Carolina, Charlotte developed a revolutionary prefabrication technique for the passive/active wall system. Exterior walls are 6 in. of Styrofoam® insulation sandwiched between layers of geopolymer cement concrete (GCC). The wall provides thermal mass and functions as a cooling system.

Traditional concrete uses portland cement as a binding agent, but the students used a fly-ash recipe instead. The result is a more environmentally friendly substance that creates less air pollution and carbon emissions during manufacturing. Portland cement is fired in kilns at very high temperatures, releasing harmful carbon in the process. The geopolymer needs heating to cure, but does not require firing in a kiln. The students said their mixture reduces carbon emissions by 90% compared to concrete.

Mats of small-diameter plastic capillary tubes are embedded in the precast panels. In warm weather, the concrete walls extract interior heat; at night, water in the capillaries is pumped through heat exchangers, where the heat is expelled into the night air. The combination of the large interior concrete surfaces and the embedded tubes creates an efficient way to transfer heat from the interior of the house to the exterior. This system cools the concrete and, therefore, the interior space. The tubes create a way of passively cooling the house without the need for compressors or refrigerants.

The dining table fits into the kitchen island to provide extra counter space or can be pulled out as a dining table for eight.

triple glazing, argon gas fills, and two low-E coatings that deliver insulation values of R-8. Besides their excellent insulation, the windows and glass provide soundproofing and block drafts.

Solar panels above the roof are on an adjustable rack so they can be moved out over the deck to provide summer shading to the exterior rooms and to the southern wall. The panels can be retracted in winter to allow the sun to passively heat and light the home through the southern glass wall.

ADAPTABLE FURNISHINGS

To maximize space in the house, some of the furnishings can be reconfigured for different purposes. The dining table stores under the kitchen counter to open up floor space. When it's pulled out it seats eight people for dinner. The entertainment center opens to reveal a Murphy bed for guests. Living room furniture can be moved outside to create a sitting area for relaxing and watching television.

The house won the People's Choice Award in the 2013 Solar Decathlon and came in third place for engineering. After the event, the house was transported back to the Charlotte campus, where it sits in crates awaiting reconstruction.

TOP: The hinged entertainment center is a unique design. The television can be watched in the living room in the usual way or pivoted for viewing from the deck. A hidden Murphy bed behind the TV wall can be pulled down for guests (see the top photo on p. 57).

BOTTOM: The entertainment center opens up to the deck. Indoor furniture can also be moved for outdoor living.

FACING PAGE TOP: With the Murphy bed in use, the entertainment center panel provides some privacy for overnight guests.

FACING PAGE BOTTOM: The shower drain is incorporated into the flooring system so no barrier or enclosure is needed. Privacy is provided by the wall of greenery surrounding the deck. The faucets are low flow.

The recycled steel post and beams provide a structure for the house, PV panels, and a vertical garden.

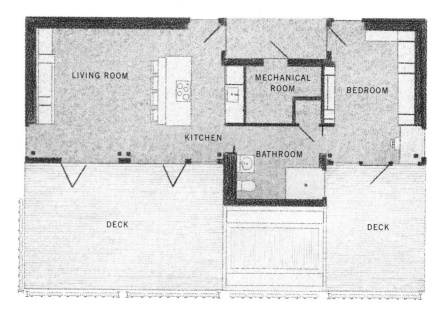

GREEN FEATURES
- Bamboo paneling
- Dual-flush toilets
- Low-flow faucets and showers
- Low- or no-VOC finishes
- Recycled materials
- Vertical garden
- Rainwater collection

ENERGY-EFFICIENT FEATURES
- Passive solar orientation
- Movable PV panels
- High-performance glass
- Triple-pane windows
- ERV
- Mini-split heat pumps
- Efficient heat pump water heater
- Insulated precast concrete panels
- Thermally modified ash flooring
- Capillary tubes
- LED and CFL lighting
- ENERGY STAR–rated appliances
- Interactive energy management system

INTERACTIVE ENERGY MANAGEMENT

Studies show that people who receive direct feedback on their power consumption reduce their electricity use in the home. The design team for UrbanEden developed a program for a Microsoft® Surface™ tablet PC that lets occupants monitor an array of house information, such as interior temperatures, operation of the capillary tube system (in the walls and roof), energy consumption, PV energy generation, and streaming video feeds from the home's multiple security cameras. The program can also control some operations in the home, such as thermostat settings, water heater mode selection, lighting, and PV array rack movement.

The systems are enabled by two programmable automation controllers, which operate and monitor the capillary tube system, where sensors embedded in the walls regulate temperature changes in the house. A third controller moves the PV panel rack back and forth over the house following the sun's movement.

Two other systems, The Nexia™ Home Intelligence package and the Powerhouse Dynamics eMonitor™ (since renamed SiteSage®), enable many home functions to be operated remotely, such as turning on or off devices plugged into wall outlets and adjusting the thermostat set point. Control commands and data monitoring are accessible on the tablet PC.

Sensors mounted to a circuit within the home's main service panel measure and record the building's energy consumption and energy generation. That data is sent over the Internet to Powerhouse Dynamic servers, where they're analyzed, tabulated, and graphed into a useful format. The tables and graphs are accessible on the web. Powerhouse Dynamic software can also provide energy conservation tips. For more information on this system, visit the UrbanEden website (urbaneden.uncc.edu/house/engineering/control-system).

LAKEVIEW HOUSE

SIPs

PHOTOGRAPHER
Connie J. Reinert

ARCHITECT
Domain Architecture
and Design

MANUFACTURER
EPS Buildings

BLOWER DOOR TEST
1.36 air changes per
hour @ 50 Pascals
(1.36 ACH@50Pascals)

HOME ENERGY RATING
SYSTEM (HERS®) INDEX
–4 (see Glossary on
p. 222)

LOCATION
Gilmore City, Iowa

SIZE
860 sq. ft.

MORE THAN 90,000 VISITORS WALKED THROUGH
the Lakeview House at the Home and Garden Show at the Minneapolis Convention Center in 2011. The design of this modest home demonstrated the energy efficiency and generous living space that could be accomplished in a mere 860 sq. ft. Because Minnesota is often called the Land of 10,000 Lakes, the design was named Lakeview. The house incorporates large, tall windows and walk-out patios to accommodate lake living, extending its small footprint to the surrounding landscape.

SITED WITH FARM VIEWS

The plan was to sell the home to an interested buyer at the conclusion of the show. And that's just what happened. Carolyn Ricklefs bought the house and had it erected in rural Gilmore City, Iowa—with a farm view, rather than a lake view. The sights from the house are of rolling pastures and a creek. It was strategically located on the rural property to take advantage of the warm southern sun for the cold winters of the upper Great Plains, which also allows the owner to enjoy the view through the large doors and windows.

BUILDING WITH SIPS

The SIP walls are 6½ in. thick and provide an R-26 insulation rating. Roof panels are 10½ in. thick for a very snug R-40 rating. A 3-ft. overhang protects the house from the weather and limits the solar gain from the high sun of summer. Insulated concrete forms (ICFs) were used for the foundation, increasing the efficiency of the overall envelope of the house. To achieve the –4 HERS rating, manufacturer EPS Buildings used special computer software to account for the R-values of the panels and the effects of the home's passive-solar design.

To achieve the best effects of passive energy, the house was sited so the living areas have a southern exposure. That orientation offers excellent daylighting and beautiful views of the creek, pastures, fields, and gardens.

According to Carolyn, the house is very comfortable in all seasons. In the winter, the large windows allow warmth from the sun to enter, while the SIPs hold in heat and reduce airflow from outside to the interior. The cost of heating in the coldest winter months is $55 to $65, which is very low for this Midwest location (or for nearly any house in nearly any heating climate).

With its energy efficiency, low maintenance, and comfortable living space, the house is perfect for a single homeowner or couple. Even though it has a petite footprint, the indoor–outdoor space and airy, light interior make it feel much more expansive.

Windows on the south and west walls bring in added light, decrease the need for electrical lighting, and give the house a more spacious feel.

LED: THE NEWEST GENERATION OF LIGHTS

A light-emitting diode (LED) is a semiconductor device that emits visible light when an electric current passes through it. LED lights are more energy efficient, more durable, and longer lasting (about 25 times longer lasting) than both incandescent and compact fluorescent lights. LED bulbs that have ENERGY STAR qualification are required to replicate the experience of a standard incandescent A-type bulb. With incandescent lights phasing out and the cost of LED lights falling, their use in homes is on the rise.

The new LEDs can be dimmed and retrofitted into existing fixtures. Some smart bulbs can be controlled by smart phones to dim or go on or off at a particular time. According to one LED bulb manufacturer, Cree®, their "LED bulbs save 84 percent of the energy compared to typical incandescent bulbs, are designed to last 25 times longer, and come with an industry-leading 10-year limited warranty."

TOP: The bedroom on the upper floor overlooks the space below and enjoys a view of the pastures.

BOTTOM: The large windows provide passive heating on the south side and allow the homeowner to enjoy the beautiful natural landscaping around the house.

The modest kitchen is open to the living and dining room areas. The appliances are ENERGY STAR–rated and the lights are all LEDs. Countertops are high-pressure laminate.

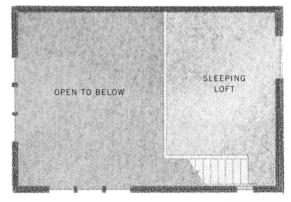

UPPER LEVEL

ENTRANCE

OPEN TO BELOW

SLEEPING LOFT

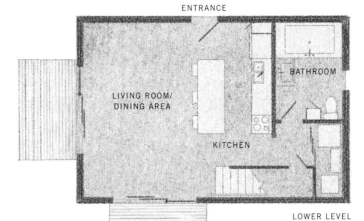

LIVING ROOM/ DINING AREA

BATHROOM

KITCHEN

LOWER LEVEL

TOP AND BOTTOM: The house was initially erected at the Minneapolis Convention Center for a home and garden show. The first panels went up at 10:00 A.M. and the structure was complete by 1:30 P.M. The house was left unfinished so visitors could see the construction components.

GREEN FEATURES
- Small footprint
- Recycled metal roof
- Water-efficient waterless tank toilets
- Low-flow showerheads
- Recycled materials
- Native plantings

ENERGY-EFFICIENT FEATURES
- Triple-pane windows
- Large overhangs
- Heat pump
- ICF foundation
- SIPs
- LED and CFL lighting
- ENERGY STAR–rated appliances
- ENERGY STAR–rated ceiling fans

RIGHT: The vinyl siding has a shakelike appearance on the upper part of the house and is clapboardlike lower down. The owner chose to alter the appearance and color of the siding to add texture and visually break up the tall south face of the home. Plantings around the house are all native and require minimal maintenance.

BELOW: After the home and garden show, the house was reerected at its current location. The foundation was built with ICFs, helping create an energy-efficient envelope. The structure went up in a few days in the rural area of Gilmore City, Iowa, and was completed in two months.

WHAT ARE STRUCTURAL INSULATED PANELS?

SIPs are energy efficient, make homes more comfortable, and can be installed quickly, which explains why this construction method is growing in popularity. Most SIPs are sandwiches of rigid foam chemically bonded between two OSB or plywood panels. Some are available with metal in place of boards.

Panels join together using long, interlocking strips of wood, called splines, to create an airtight barrier for roofing, siding, or flooring. Routed channels, or chases, are cut into the panels for wiring and cables. Window and door openings are generally cut out of the panels in the factory. For houses with high R-values or big openings, headers can be precut and insulated with SIPs in the factory. Panels can be created that are up to 24 ft. sq. Depending on their size, panels are hoisted into place on site with the help of a lift or crane. Houses can be designed using an AutoCAD® program and the panels cut using a computer-run machine or computer numerical control (CNC) machine (see p. 68). The panels are numbered and quickly erected on site.

EPS Buildings—a partner in the ENERGY STAR program and a member of the National Association of Home Builders (NAHB®) energy program—manufactured the panels for the Lakeview House. For additional information, see their website (epsbuildings.com).

LITTLE HOUSE ON THE FERRY

CLT Components

PHOTOGRAPHERS
Trent Bell (except
where noted)

ARCHITECT
GO Logic

BUILDER
C. W. Conway and Sons

MANUFACTURER
Nordic Structures

ENGINEERING
Bensonwood®

LOCATION
City Point, Vinalhaven,
Maine

SIZE
980 sq. ft.

A SLOPING SITE ADJACENT TO AN OLD GRANITE quarry with expansive ocean views, on an island an hour's ferry ride from Rockland, Maine, is the perfect location for a seasonal getaway.

The residence consists of three small structures—a living unit and two bedroom units that are linked by an exterior deck. The units follow the land's topography and are arranged to create a loosely enclosed outdoor space that can be accessed from multiple points. The owners, Nadja and Nicholas van Praag, chose this location for its privacy, intimacy, and natural beauty—a large portion of the site where the cabins sit has exposed rocks and ledges with spectacular views.

Nadja and Nicholas initially refurbished a house on Vinalhaven Island. When the house on the adjacent lot went on the market, they purchased it, removed the structure, and built the new cabins in its place. They continue to use their older house and reserve the Little House on the Ferry for guests. The couple's primary residence is in Vienna, Austria, and they plan to use their Maine retreat mostly in the summer and early fall.

MULTIPLE STRUCTURES

By separating one residence into three independent small structures, the cabins sit as lightly as possible on the terrain without disrupting the site. Nadja and Nicholas also prefer the flexibility and privacy of separate structures. And because they use the home only in warmer months, walking outside from one cabin to another is not an issue. (This type of arrangement would clearly not be practical in such a cold environment if the house were used year round.)

USING CROSS-LAMINATED TIMBER PREFABRICATED COMPONENTS

Architect GO Logic recommended using cross-laminated timber (CLT; see p. 69) as a method of prefabricating portions of the building because it would reduce construction time and require no interior finishes. The panels were erected on site in just four days, and the house was ready for occupancy in about six months. During that time, electrical and plumbing hookups were completed, siding and roofing materials were installed, and a bit of customization was done by the owners—all using local labor.

Because the home is used only in the summer and early fall, it required minimal insulation—rigid foam on the roof—and no heating system. The vintage Preway wood-burning fireplace provides all the heat needed for the months the house is in use. The sliding doors on the three structures not only provide privacy and light control but also protect the house from the elements when the owners are away.

The three cabins, connected by a walkway, sit comfortably on the rocky terrain at different levels to maximize views and minimize disturbance to the land. The roofing is metal standing seam and the siding is eastern white cedar which will weather to a natural gray.

Photo courtesy of GO Logic

The main cabin includes space for living and dining and a kitchen. The wood fireplace in the living room is a vintage Preway, vented out the roof.

TOP: On each of the three structures, sliding screens close off the sliding glass doors to provide privacy and light control while also protecting them from the elements in winter months. The sliding screens park adjacent to the openings, and the screen slats align with the siding so that when the panels are closed they blend in.

BOTTOM: The cabins sit among beautiful evergreens and look out onto Hurricane Sound and Penobscot Bay.

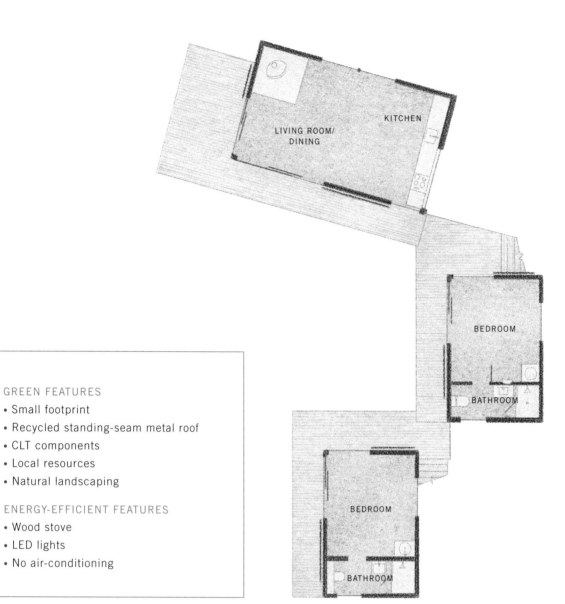

LIVING ROOM/
DINING

KITCHEN

BEDROOM

BATHROOM

BEDROOM

BATHROOM

GREEN FEATURES
• Small footprint
• Recycled standing-seam metal roof
• CLT components
• Local resources
• Natural landscaping

ENERGY-EFFICIENT FEATURES
• Wood stove
• LED lights
• No air-conditioning

A CNC machine in action.

Photo courtesy of Nordic Structures

COMPUTER NUMERICAL CONTROL MACHINES

CNC refers to the computer control of machine tools for manufacturing parts in metal, wood, or plastic. CNC machines are fed digital designs and cutting instructions and, from these plan instructions, the machines manufacture products without paper ever touching a drafting table. The machines cut curved and straight pieces faster and more accurately than can be achieved with less sophisticated cutting tools. The digital designs, which can be used over and over indefinitely, instruct the machine to create single or multiple cuts, in several directions and at varying depths at the same time.

The flooring in the main part of the cabin is CLT, which was sanded and painted. The kitchen flooring is laminate.

CLT COMPONENTS

The CLT components used to construct the cabins were prefabricated in Chantiers Chibougamau, a factory in Quebec. The panels are layers of solid black spruce laminated together at right angles to each other, under pressure, in the same way that plywood is made. This process creates panels that are structurally and dimensionally stable. Panels can be fabricated as large as 8 ft. by 64 ft. and up to 1 ft. thick.

CLT panels offer positive environmental benefits, including carbon storage and low greenhouse emissions during manufacturing, and they are recyclable. The panels reduce construction time compared to some other building methods and require a shorter learning curve for installers. Another advantage of CLT panels is that they can be exposed to the weather on the exterior and can also be used as interior surfaces.

For Little House on the Ferry, CLT panels form the entire enclosure for the cabins—floors, walls, and roofs— and function as both structure and finish to create a minimalist and rustic appearance. The panels were precut using computer-controlled milling machinery, a technology called CNC (see "Computer Numerical Control Machines" on the facing page). Shop drawings from Bensonwood provided the size, shape, and orientation of each panel. The sequence of packing, unloading, and erecting the panels was carefully choreographed on site. The CLT components reduce on-site labor and can efficiently be assembled on diverse sites—an excellent solution for building structures in remote locations such as rural Maine.

SU+RE
HOUSE

Modular

PHOTOGRAPHERS
Juan Alicante (except where noted)

**ARCHITECT/BUILDER/
MANUFACTURER/
INTERIOR DESIGNER**
Students from Stevens
Institute of Technology

BLOWER DOOR TEST
0.60 ACH50 (target for
final install)

LOCATION
2015 Solar Decathlon,
Irvine, Calif.

SIZE
997 sq. ft.

THE SU+RE HOUSE TEAM FROM STEVENS INSTITUTE of Technology built this house to reduce their "contribution to climate change while bracing for its effects." This is the school's third Solar Decathlon entry, and the house was as timely as any in the October 2015 event in Irvine, Calif.

The house was built to withstand major storms, and PV panels were installed to provide electricity and hot water when power is lost; the panels begin producing as soon as the sun returns. Other innovations include protecting against flooding and cutting-edge insulation and air sealing.

THE TEAM GOALS

The SU+RE House prototype addresses the need for sustainable and resilient homes in East Coast communities along the New Jersey and New York shorelines, which are at great risk of rising sea levels and damaging storms. The house was inspired by the devastation caused by 2012's Hurricane Sandy, which directly affected residents of the metropolitan area as well as some students involved in this project.

The house is designed to be built at a lower height than the design flood elevation (DFE) designated by the Federal Emergency Management Agency (FEMA), and the National Flood Insurance Program (NFIP). Keeping the building low to the ground also maintains architectural traditions of the area, reduces the cost of building on stilts, and makes the house accessible to the elderly and handicapped, who would have difficulty climbing to the recommended flood-protection heights. To build at lower elevations, the team designed a protective building envelope that would endure a massive storm.

A WATERPROOF, DEBRIS-RESISTANT BARRIER

In addition to operable shutters on the south facade and "removable plugs" (designed by the students) around the windows and doors, the house is raised just above grade, and exterior sheathing produces a waterproof barrier. The team used marine construction techniques, such as durable plastic panels laminated to standard home sheathing. A structural adhesive typically used below the waterline in marine applications was applied to the sheathing between the panels. This bond creates an impenetrable seal, protecting the lower part of the house up to the local designated flood height regulations. To further seal the envelope of the house, rubber gaskets are used between moving parts, such as on the storm shutters.

The front, south exposure of the house has large overhangs that include the "storm shutters" that shade the house in the open position and can be lowered to protect it from water, debris, and vandalism during a devastating storm.

The main living space of the home opens onto the large south deck. Pale-colored birch ceiling panels, light colored maple flooring, and built-in birch cabinetry do their part to maintain the bright and airy feeling of the space.

TOP: In addition to the interior door (shown), the bathroom also has an entrance from the southern deck, so it can function as a mudroom to prevent sand being dragged through the house when a family member or guest returns from the beach.

BOTTOM: This wide-open space contains room for the living, entertaining, cooking, and eating areas. The kitchen features ENERGY STAR–rated appliances and efficient LED lighting. Inductive charging elements are integrated into the countertops to allow homeowners to charge cell phones simply by laying them on the counter. The charging station is connected to the home's resilient solar array, so even in a power outage, phones can charge (as long as the sun is shining).

The operable storm shutters are secured open above the deck area on the south side of the house. Made of TruGrain™, a composite product, the deck can be used for relaxing outside and for expanding the interior living space.

REDUCING ENERGY CONSUMPTION

The Stevens Institute of Technology team used the German Passive House Planning Package (PHPP) software modeling tool (see the Glossary on p. 222) to make design decisions regarding window configuration, exterior envelope R-values, and mechanical systems. As a result of several innovative techniques, the SU+RE House meets those passive house energy and air-tightness requirements.

Before determining how much energy the solar panels would need to supply, the team reduced the house's demand for energy by about 91% over the average New Jersey house. Much of that reduction was achieved by increased insulation. The walls, floors, and ceilings are filled with mineral wool batt insulation. Mineral wool batts are installed on the inside face of the walls, and mineral wool board covers the exterior wall sheathing. Additional sloped polyisocyanurate foam insulation over the roof creates a triple-layer of insulation.

Careful air sealing, using all-acrylic tapes and specialty membranes, ensured a very tight envelope. Triple-pane high-performance windows and an ERV system reduce energy consumption further. The ERV preconditions incoming air to maintain healthy indoor air quality while retaining interior temperatures.

Use of high-efficiency appliances, LED lighting, and a high-efficiency hot water system further reduce energy use. A high-efficiency heat pump heats, cools, and dehumidifies the house. The system is zoned so that temperature can be controlled individually, room by room.

When the weather gets hot, the house has well-designed solar shading on the south face, which blocks the heat of the midday sun. A combination of a shutter and louver system keeps out the high summer sun but allows the lower sun to enter during the winter months. Without well-planned shading, a home with as much glass as this could quickly become too hot.

RIGHT TOP AND BOTTOM: Two small bedrooms tucked into the house's north side are thickly insulated and have operable triple-glazed windows, which reduce energy needs even during the coldest part of a New Jersey winter.

THERMAL BRIDGING

A good deal of energy can be lost through the envelope of a house at the corners, at seams where two different materials meet, and at windows and doors. This heat loss is called *thermal bridging*, a break in the insulation layer where heat can flow more easily from the inside of a space to the outside (or from the outside to the inside) through a material with higher conductivity or lower thermal resistance. This process can reduce the overall thermal performance of the house, leading to higher energy use and cold spots on the interior, which can cause condensation and mold.

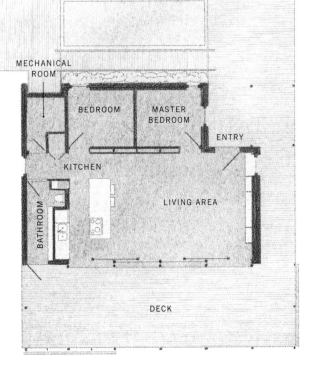

The house was originally erected near the school campus in New Jersey and overlooks the Manhattan skyline.

Photo courtesy of author

GREEN FEATURES

- Cedar-shingle siding rainscreen
- Fiber-composite storm shutters
- Vacuum-infused glass-fiber panels
- Composite decking and louvers
- Flood-proof wall and floor assemblies
- GREENGUARD-certified kitchen materials
- Dual-flush toilets
- Low-flow faucets and showers
- Low- or no-VOC finishes
- FSC-certified wood

ENERGY-EFFICIENT FEATURES

- PV electric solar hot water system
- Rooftop and building-integrated PV panels
- Triple-pane argon-filled windows
- Integrated solar shading
- Large overhangs
- ERV
- Mini-split system with zone control
- Triple-layer mineral wool insulation (R-38 walls)
- Airtight construction
- LED lighting
- ENERGY STAR–rated appliances

BUILDING-INTEGRATED PHOTOVOLTAICS

The house has two PV systems, one on the rooftop and one on the south-facing operable shutters. These two arrays provide enough power to supply the home's energy needs and hot water throughout the year.

Instead of using bulky, heavy glass PV panels that are typically attached to a roof rack, the team used a lighter, more adaptable system. The panels are attached to the flood-resistant storm shutters, without inhibiting the shutters' operation. The panels collect sunlight when the shutters are in the open position to make energy for hot water.

During a storm, shutters are lowered to protect the house from heavy rain and flying debris. If a panel is damaged, it can easily be repaired or replaced, rather than replacing the entire system.

AN INNOVATIVE HOT WATER SYSTEM

The team developed a domestic hot water system that is sustainable and resilient. In most systems, the standard device that converts solar energy to usable house current can become disabled in a storm, so the students developed a different system that ensures hot water even when the house is detached from the grid. The innovation combines a PV electric hot water system and an integrated heat pump hot water heater.

The cost of the components and installation of PV systems makes them cost-competitive alternatives to solar thermal collectors. The simplicity and durability of PV electric systems also present operation and maintenance advantages over solar hot water systems.

Solar energy generated by the PV system is transferred as direct current to the PV heater control unit and the heating element. The PV heater delivers maximum heating energy to the domestic hot water tank. This system is coupled with a back-up high-efficiency heat pump, which is activated only when the sun cannot provide enough energy to keep the water temperature above a set point.

Even in heat pump mode, the hot water system still uses 70% less energy than a standard electric hot water heater. The system's greatest benefit is that the flow of electricity and energy it produces provides power to the home when the sun is shining, even when disconnected from the grid. Unlike traditional PV systems, this one does not rely on the grid to collect and distribute energy. In addition, the SU+RE House system is not only more cost-effective but is also more durable and requires less maintenance.

A RESILIENT POWER SYSTEM

Houses along the shore are vulnerable to frequent power outages because of regular harsh storms. The SU+RE House can be tied to the grid and produce about 10,000 watts of electricity in its sustainable everyday mode. When the array is disconnected from the grid in its resiliency mode, the transformer-less inverter switches to the 3,000 watts of standby power available to the homeowner via charging stations and outlets throughout the house. This power is available only when the sun is out.

To help the community during a blackout, the house has a charging hub on the exterior so neighbors without power can charge their electric devices.

This house serves as a wonderful, pragmatic solution for residences near the shore. The Stevens Institute of Technology team scored well at the 2015 Solar Decathlon, winning first place in 7 out of 10 categories as well as first place overall. When the house returns from the West Coast, it will be used as a learning center in Hoboken, N.J., at the Stevens Institute.

BAYVIEW COTTAGE

Modular

PHOTOGRAPHER
Alison Caron Design

ARCHITECT
Union Studio Architects/
Community Design

DEVELOPERS/BUILDERS
Cape Built Development
MS Ocean View

MANUFACTURER
Keiser Homes

INTERIOR DESIGNER
Angela Hamway
Mackenzie & Mae

LOCATION
Dennis Port, Mass.

SIZE
1,027 sq. ft.

BAYVIEW COTTAGE IS PART OF A COTTAGE

community overlooking Nantucket Sound. The community was built in clusters of cottages around common areas, creating the opportunity for smaller "neighborhoods within the neighborhood" so characteristic of traditional seaside seasonal communities. Developer Rob Brennan comments that in building Cape Cod's first oceanfront cottage colony in more than 50 years, "We focused as much on community fabric as we did on our cottage architecture. Porches front onto common greens, and walkways connect neighbors with one another . . . and [become] the setting for coffee drop-ins and spontaneous evening gatherings." The cottages share a private 650-ft. beach, mooring, pool, gym, and clubhouse on 8 acres.

SMALL BUT SPACIOUS
Like all five models built in the 63-cottage community, the Bayview Cottage feels spacious despite its small footprint. The efficient use of space includes minimal hallways and a shiplike use of traditionally "leftover" spaces for bookcases, nooks, and small closets.

High ceilings are another significant feature that allows the homes to live larger than the footprints suggest. "The living spaces were carefully designed to be comfortable but not bigger than needed to be functional," according to architect Douglas Kallfelz. "I think people are surprised by how livable these cottages are . . . even though, by the numbers, the rooms are significantly smaller than they are used to seeing. It is very gratifying to see people come around to the notion that they can live with less than they expected . . . and it isn't really a compromise."

BUILDING PREFAB
Kallfelz and the development team were convinced that this project was a perfect opportunity to leverage the value of prefab construction. Building the components in a fully controlled interior environment would help ensure that the quality of the construction would be high and that the impact on the environment of this exposed coastal site would be minimized. In addition, because the site was very tight, prefab construction was a good solution since there was limited need for the extensive staging and material storage areas that are typically required during on-site construction.

Once delivered, the prefabricated modules for each cottage are set quickly (typically in a single afternoon), so disturbance to the existing residents is minimal when a new home is erected. Kallfelz points out that in addition to the other advantages, the carrying costs for the construction

A porch on the ground level and off the upstairs front bedroom provide places to enjoy the beach environment and casual interaction with neighbors. The permeable crushed-shell walkways allow water to seep back into the ground. Cedar shingle siding creates an attractive New England appearance and offers natural insulation properties.

Windows on all sides allow a good deal of light into the living area. On cool days the gas fireplace supplements the heating system. Ottomans under the windows can be rolled out into the living space for extra seating.

are much lower than in conventional construction. This is an important cost saver since the time span from the owner's decision to buy to their move in is significantly shorter than in a conventional stick-built construction process.

BUILT TO HANDLE THE ELEMENTS

We've all seen the damage wrought by hurricanes and other coastal storms. The cottages in this community were designed and constructed to exceed the 110-mph wind zone provisions of the

ABOVE: A small oak table in a niche just off the mudroom is the perfect spot to drop off the car keys (so owners and guests can switch to their bikes when they arrive). The basket is there to catch sandy towels after lazy afternoons on the neighborhood beach.

FACING PAGE BOTTOM: The kitchen in this small house is surprisingly spacious, and the white color palette maintains the airy look of the rest of the interior. The wood laminate floors are 74% preconsumer recycled wood fiber and chips from sustainable sources.

TOP: The cottage was designed to give potential buyers the opportunity to visualize mixing treasured family pieces with new items for an updated airy look. The chandelier in the dining room is from a consignment shop and was given a new look with a fresh coat of white paint. The chest, repurposed from a local vintage furniture dealer, was chosen to provide additional storage for table linens, candles, and so forth.

BOTTOM: Windows in the master bedroom open onto a view of the ocean. The air source heat pump (at left) both heats and cools the house.

The modular sections of the house were built in Maine and took just 15 weeks to complete on site. (By contrast, a typical site-built house would probably take about a year to build and be far less efficient in terms of materials and energy.)

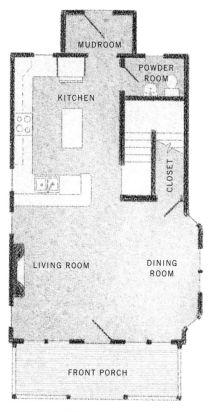

FIRST FLOOR

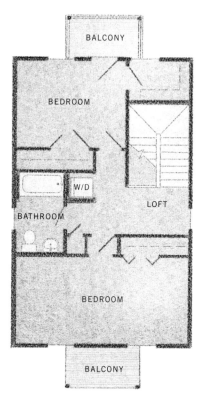

SECOND FLOOR

GREEN FEATURES
- Composite decking with recycled content
- Low-VOC carpeting
- Hurricane-rated windows
- Impact-resistant glass
- House exceeds 110-mph wind zone provisions
- Permeable crushed-shell walkways
- Bluestone gravel driveways
- Locally sourced materials
- Modular construction to minimize product waste

ENERGY-EFFICIENT FEATURES
- High-efficiency air-to-air heat pumps for heating and cooling (see "Modern Heat Pump Mini- and Multi-Split Systems" on p. 129)
- Dense-packed cellulose insulation
- LED and CFL lighting
- ENERGY STAR–rated appliances
- ENERGY STAR–rated tankless water heater
- ENERGY STAR–rated ceiling fans

Massachusetts Building Code and FEMA's *Coastal Construction Manual*.

Windows are hurricane rated and even pass Florida's "large missile" impact test, which simulates the damage of wind-borne debris by using a 6-ft.-long 2×4 fired from a pneumatic cannon. As an added benefit, the same windows that stand up to hurricane-force winds also provide significant soundproofing against both occasional howling gales and spirited games of beach volleyball.

Cedar shingles on the exterior not only maintain the Cape Cod tradition but also hold up well and keep their natural insulation properties in saltwater environments. The asphalt roof shingles were chosen for their high wind rating.

The houses in the community were built to the Seasonal Resort Community zoning bylaw, which was drafted by Dennis, Mass., Town Planner Daniel Fortier, with input from land owners, developers, neighboring residents, and local businesses. The group's objective was to craft zoning that would offer an alternative to oceanfront McMansions on 1-acre lots by allowing higher density development of smaller-scale second homes in the same way that families have called Dennis Port oceanfront cottages their "place on the Cape" for generations.

The bylaw allows owners to occupy their cottages from April 1 to October 31, as well as four days per month throughout the winter. This bolsters the local economy but avoids overpopulating local schools. Cottages at Heritage Sands range from one to three bedrooms and are priced from $400,000 to $900,000. For additional information about the Heritage Sands community, visit their website (heritagesands.com).

The community sits directly on Nantucket Sound in Dennis Port, a village where some of Cape Cod's first "cottage colonies" evolved from army tent compounds starting in the 1930s. The Bayview Cottage is one of several models offered.

POCKET COMMUNITIES

Pocket communities make up small clusters of houses in urban, suburban, or rural settings in which small-footprint homes are arranged around a shared common area. This closeness encourages interaction among neighbors and is perfect for people who seek a stronger sense of community than is found in a conventional neighborhood. Although the houses are generally close together, they are designed to provide privacy by use of careful window placement and individual gates or gardens that designate private spaces. Parking is usually located away from the individual houses, so residents must walk through the common areas to get to their homes.

SOLAR LANEWAY HOUSE

SIPs

PHOTOGRAPHER
Colin Perry

DESIGNER/BUILDER
Lanefab Design/Build

MANUFACTURER
Insulspan

CERTIFICATIONS
EnerGuide 90 (see
p. 89)

LOCATION
Vancouver, B.C., Canada

SIZE
1,050 sq. ft.

PETTO CHAN AND HIS WIFE, BILLIE LEUNG, SPENT many weekends looking at homes in Vancouver. They were living in his parents' basement with their young daughter and wanted a place of their own. Their priorities included a home close to their work so they'd need only one car and office space for the many days Petto worked at home.

Because she teaches baking in a high school, Billie craved a large kitchen, so she could use her baking skills at home for family and friends. Both she and Petto wanted a modern home that was small so they wouldn't spend their time and money maintaining it.

CHOOSING A HOUSE

After looking at more than a hundred houses, the couple realized that they would not find what they wanted in terms of design or efficiency on their $800,000 budget in this area, where houses typically start at $1 million. One advantage of building a laneway house (see the sidebar on p. 87) was that all their money would go toward construction, rather than land. At that point, building in his parents' backyard became a more attractive option. Not only could they build a house with the exact design they wanted, but they'd also still be able to enjoy his mom's cooking on weekday evenings.

Before they applied for a permit or looked for a builder, they made sure they had a clear vision of what their laneway home would look like. First, it would be small but spacious. Instead of many small rooms they opted for fewer larger rooms. Instead of a formal dining room, they wanted a large kitchen where the three of them could eat at the kitchen island.

The house would also be very energy efficient. The 13-in.-thick walls include 6½-in. SIPs and several inches of rock wool insulation in the inner service wall (which houses the wiring, plumbing, ducts, and fire sprinkler piping). PV panels on the roof provide all the energy required during the mildest months of the year, with only a small amount of additional energy needed for the colder months. The house is net zero energy for many months of the year, with monthly winter bills running about $80. Appliances are ENERGY STAR-rated and lights are all LED.

TRACKING THE ENERGY

The house's performance continues to be monitored by Enlighten Manager, a tracking program from Enphase Energy®, that offers continuous data on the energy produced by the PV panels. After the first year and a half, the Solar Laneway House's PV panels had produced 4.2 megawatt hours of power, saving the homeowners about $1,500 in energy costs.

The living space is wrapped in a highly efficient envelope of SIPs and triple-pane windows. The siding is cedar, stucco, and bluestone, with accents of fiber cement.

ABOVE: Appliances in the kitchen are ENERGY STAR rated, all lights are LEDs, and countertops are quartz. The staircase (to the left) is sectioned off with glass, instead of a solid wall, to provide a more open feeling to the area and to shed light on the treads.

RIGHT: The living room is open to the kitchen and dining areas. Flooring throughout most of the first floor consists of a 4-in. slab of concrete topped with a thin layer of finished decorative concrete, which provides thermal mass and requires minimal maintenance.

TOP: The modern black-and-white upstairs bathroom has an opaque glass door, which allows extra light into the room while still providing privacy. The single trough sink is wide enough for two people to use side by side.

BOTTOM: The office and child's room are tucked away off the main living space at the side of the house.

LANEWAY HOUSES

Laneway houses are small-scale, fully independent homes that are typically built in the backyard of an existing single-family home. The houses often are located where a garage once stood, just off the rear alley, or lane, hence the name *laneway*. They were first approved in Vancouver, B.C., in 2009 thanks to the city's EcoDensity policy.

Although they've been built in other Canadian cities, laneway houses are mostly found in Vancouver because it has such a large network of lanes. In 2009 when the law was enacted, about 59,000 houses were determined to be suited for laneway units. To date, the popular program has issued more than 1,600 permits. Extensive rules govern the size, shape, and location of the houses. Other, more practical issues also fall within laneway regulations that oversee parking, the issuing of addresses (which could get complicated with two separate houses on the same lot), landscaping, and sewer and water connections.

As a result of the laneway boom, the lane areas, which previously were often neglected, have become revitalized while providing expanded housing options for people who want to live in the city. Just as the city planned, this construction has added density to communities without construction of multistory apartment houses.

Laneway houses are a subcategory of accessory dwelling units (ADUs), which can also include basement dwellings, apartments over a garage, and additional houses on an existing lot where a house already exists. Regulations for all of these units are specified by the state or province. In Vancouver, laneway houses must be sold with the original house but can be rented or occupied by family members.

The size of the house depends on the size of the lot, although the houses are typically between 500 sq. ft. and 1,000 sq. ft. The maximum height for a laneway house is 20 ft. and 1½ stories (which means the second floor has to be smaller than the ground floor to reduce the apparent size of the structure).

Laneway houses (and other ADUs) offer an alternative type of housing for people who do not want to live in an apartment building but either cannot afford or do not need a full-size single-family house. For additional information about laneway houses in Vancouver, visit the city's website (vancouver.ca/home-property-development/laneway-houses-and-secondary-suites.aspx).

DRAIN WATER
HEAT RECOVERY

In most houses a great deal of energy is lost when the warm water from showering goes down the drain. According to Energy Saver (energy. gov/energysaver/tips-water-heating), "Water heating is the second largest energy expense in your home. It typically accounts for about 18% of your utility bill after heating and cooling."

A drain water heat recovery system captures heat from graywater (usually from the shower) and uses it to supplement the water heater, cutting down on energy required to obtain hot water. The recovered heat also expands the amount of hot water available in the home so that the last person showering won't run out of hot water. The house then consumes less energy, so energy bills decrease. For further information about the system used in the Solar Laneway House, visit the Watercycles™ website (www. watercycles.ca)

The wallpaper and drawings in the small downstairs powder room lend an air of whimsy.

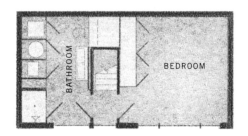

SECOND FLOOR

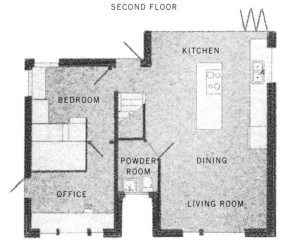

FIRST FLOOR

GREEN FEATURES
- Locally sourced cedar siding, windows, and panels
- Dual-flush toilets
- Low-flow faucets and showers
- Low/no-VOC paint and adhesives
- HRV

ENERGY-EFFICIENT FEATURES
- PV panels
- Triple-pane windows and doors
- High-efficiency heat pump
- Drain water heat recovery system
- Heat pump hot water tank
- SIPs
- EPS foam
- LED lighting
- ENERGY STAR–rated appliances

Solar panels on the roof are visible from the rear of the house.
The sliding glass doors open to the kitchen.

ENERGUIDE RATING

The Canadian EnerGuide rating measures a home's energy performance so that current and future owners will know fairly precisely how energy efficient the structure is. An approved EnerGuide adviser certifies the energy performance rating.

The home's energy-efficiency level is rated on a scale of 0 to 100. An uninsulated house with significant air leaks would have a rating of 0 and a high energy consumption. A typical new home in Vancouver is built to an EnerGuide 76 rating. The Solar Laneway House has an energy rating of 90, which means it is energy efficient. Houses with a rating of 91 to 100 are often off the grid. For additional information about this program, visit the Natural Resources Canada website (www.nrcan.gc.ca/energy/efficiency/housing/new-homes/5035).

M2 CABIN

Modular

PHOTOGRAPHER
Lannie Boesinger

ARCHITECT
Balance Associates
Architects

MANUFACTURER/
BUILDER
Method Homes

LOCATION
Deming, Wash.

SIZE
1,240 sq. ft.

METHOD HOMES® HAS AN INTERESTING WAY OF selling their homes. They offer a test drive. Before finding Method online, the owners of the M2 Cabin were looking for a company that builds sustainable houses while generating minimal waste. When they contacted Method for more information, the company offered them a free weekend in one of their cabins so they could see firsthand how it "lives."

After that experience, the owners researched modular construction, knowing that the process shortened the overall duration of the building time, minimized waste, and maximized quality. Ultimately, they chose Method.

TWO MODULES DIVIDED

The house is constructed of two modules connected by a passageway. The homeowners especially like this aspect of the house, known as a dogtrot, a feature that's reminiscent of historic log cabins. It separates the living spaces from the sleeping quarters.

Setting the modules onto the foundation took place on an unusually cold mid-December day in Washington. It was completed in about seven hours. Some finish work had to be done on site after the modules were set, which took about another three weeks. In the process, some beautiful mature conifers had to be cut down, but the owners were able to maintain a good number of native Douglas firs and cedars around the perimeter. The house is in a development in the Mt. Baker foothills, where the landscaping is all natural and native to the area. Vegetation under the trees includes vine maples, elderberries, mahonia, sword ferns, trillium, salmonberries, and thimbleberries.

LIVING IN THE CABIN

Two bedrooms and a bathroom are on one side of the house, with the kitchen, dining, living, and utility room on the other. The house is private from the front and has expansive green-belt views from the back, which make this wilderness experience serene.

And it's remote, which is what the owners were looking for. Because of its location, the owners were somewhat limited in their heating and cooking options. After researching efficient heating systems, they chose propane for their stove and opted to install a mini-split ductless system, which can also function as an air-conditioner when necessary.

The two massive overhangs protect the house from the summer heat yet allow sunlight into the interior during the colder months when the sun is low in the sky. Still, the homeowners have higher electricity bills in

The two living modules are connected by a suspended passageway opened up to the outdoors by a wall of glass. One side of the house contains two bedrooms and a bathroom; the other has the kitchen, dining, living, and utility room. The siding is corrugated metal in a dark red, suggestive of a country barn. Roofing is also metal. Landscaping is native and permeable.

The living room wall opens onto a large cantilevered deck through sliding glass doors. The wood stove helps heat the house in the winter, while ENERGY STAR–rated ceiling fans keep the room feeling cool in summer.

TOP: The black steel frame, a major structural support feature of the house, functions visually as well, delineating the otherwise-open dining and living areas.

BOTTOM: The backsplash in the kitchen is durable and long-lasting metal, and the countertops are EcoTop™, an FSC-certified product made of a 50/50 fiber blend of 100% postconsumer recycled fiber and rapidly renewable bamboo fiber, bound together with a clear 100% water-based system.

Two rear cedar decks extend this small house and provide a naturally ventilated space where the home-owners can relax outside.

GREEN FEATURES

- Metal roofing/siding with recycled content
- FSC-certified maple flooring
- NAUF doors and trim
- Kitchen and bathroom countertops with recycled content
- FSC-certified wood cabinetry
- Low-flow faucets and showerheads
- Dual-flush toilets
- Low- or no-VOC paints, stains, and adhesives
- Native landscaping

ENERGY-EFFICIENT FEATURES

- Low-e coated aluminum-clad wood windows
- Ductless mini-split heating and cooling system
- Tankless water heater
- High-efficiency wood stove
- Formaldehyde-free Blown-In-Blanket® insulation with R23 walls
- ENERGY STAR–rated ceiling fans
- ENERGY STAR–rated appliances

winter than during the rest of the year because the demand for heat is high.

The owners found the whole process of building their home an engaging, creative, and fun experience. Now, they enjoy getting away from their primary residence in Seattle and appreciate the beautiful views and the skiing and hiking that are readily available from their cabin.

Sliding doors and operable clerestory windows help keep the master bedroom cool and bring the outside in, giving the space a treehouse-like feel. The mini-split system high on the wall to the left is nonintrusive and an efficient way to heat and cool the house.

HIGH-EFFICIENCY WOOD STOVES

Wood stoves are popular for many reasons. There's no smoke, minimal ash, and they do their jobs using a small amount of firewood. According to the U.S. Environmental Protection Agency (EPA), the final New Source Performance Standards (NSPS) for wood stoves will phase in emission limits over a five-year period. In the first phase, which began in spring 2015, newly manufactured wood stoves were required to meet a particulate matter (PM) emission limit of 4.5 grams of smoke per hour (g/h) for both catalytic and noncatalytic stoves. In the second phase, which will go into effect on May 15, 2020, PM emission limit will decrease to 2.0 g/h. The previous PM emission limits covered under the 1988 NSPS for catalytic stoves and noncatalytic stoves were 4.1 g/h and 7.5 g/h, respectively. Catalytic stoves are more expensive and include a honeycomb-shaped, ceramic-coated catalytic convertor combustor that burns off particles and smoke gases that pass through it.

Using a high-efficiency wood stove can significantly reduce a home's heating costs, saving resources and money. EPA-certified stoves are about 30% more efficient than the older models; compliant wood stoves carry the EPA white label.

According to Danish stove maker Morsø®, their wood stove used in the M2 Cabin was produced in a factory that gets 80% of its energy from wind, biofuel, and diesel fuel. The company also claims that 98% of the materials used to produce their stoves are from recycled materials. In addition, Morsø models are EPA approved in all 50 states, including Washington State (the nation's most strict), and are compliant with Europe's Eco Swan Label test, which goes beyond EPA testing. For additional information about regulations, visit the EPA's website (epa.gov/burnwise/woodstoves.html), and for more on the M2 Cabin's wood stove, visit Morsø's website (morso.com).

WHIDBEY ISLAND HOUSE

Timber Frame/SIPs

PHOTOGRAPHER
Dale Lang

ARCHITECT/
MANUFACTURER
FabCab

BUILDER
Jim Hall, James Hall and
Associates

LOCATION
Whidbey Island, Wash.

SIZE
1,440 sq. ft.

CAROL AND LARRY WERE READY TO DOWNSIZE TO a smaller house but wanted to remain in their town of Langley, on Whidbey Island off the coast of Washington State, where they had been living for 24 years. Their traditional 2,500-sq.-ft. home was beginning to feel too big, and they wanted something smaller and more contemporary. When a lot became available next to their daughter's house, they decided to purchase it and build their new home. Larry was already acquainted with architect Emory Baldwin of FabCab, and they approached him about building their new home.

LIVING INSIDE AND OUT

One of the owners' priorities was to build a house that would take advantage of the beautiful surrounding scenery through large windows and have easy access to outdoor living. They got what they wanted: The roof soars from 8 ft. in the front of the house to 14 ft. in the rear, adding height to the windows and offering generous light and beautiful, expansive views.

CUSTOMIZING A STANDARD PLAN

FabCab offers several basic designs that they use as-is or modify to suit clients. Carol and Larry were able to customize one of those plans to meet their design and practical requirements. Builder James Hall and Associates prepared the foundation, and then the timber frame was delivered. The frame was then enclosed with SIPs, which leave the beautiful timber frame visible inside. Windows and doors were installed in precut openings in the timber frame and SIPs. Construction of the shell to the point it was dried-in (weathertight) took about five weeks. In six months the house was complete and ready for Carol and Larry to move in.

To Larry, the heating and cooling system is one of his new home's most amazing features. "The ductless heat pump, or mini-split, is very effective and efficient. It can handle heating and cooling of our great room, and of our bedroom when we have the sliding doors open. Ceiling fans help distribute the warm air or provide a cool breeze."

DOWNSIZING AND READY FOR THE FUTURE

Carol and Larry wanted a home that would suit them not only today but also in the future. One-level living was a requirement, as were the wide doorways and a threshold-free shower in the bathroom. These and other universal design features (see the sidebar on p. 101) offered some assurance that the house would work for them into the future.

The soaring ceiling, which faces due south, rises to 14 ft. in the rear of the house, expanding the beautiful wilderness views and bringing in lots of natural light.

The owners like to open up the bedroom as wide as possible to make the home feel bigger, but typically close it off when company comes over. A translucent multipanel glass door system offers bedroom privacy while still letting in light.

CARPET TILES

Carpeting in general is not usually considered environmentally friendly, but carpet tiles can be a responsible choice. Working to keep carpeting out of landfills, several companies are introducing carpet tiles. The FLOR® tiles used in the Whidbey Island House are manufactured from 100% recycled materials. The company offers a "return and recycle program," in which they pay for the return of the tiles when they've outlived their useful life and recycle the fibers and backing. To make replacement simple, the carpet tiles are attached to each other, rather than to the floor, so the flooring beneath is not damaged and the tiles can be removed or replaced one at a time. Carpet tiles come in a multitude of colors and textures so homeowners can personalize and install their own flooring. They can be used for wall-to-wall carpeting, runners, or rugs. For more information, visit FLOR's website (flor.com).

According to Carol, "Downsizing turned out to be easier than we thought. We lost about 1,000 sq. ft., but our FabCab feels spacious and roomy. While our three kids were at home in the previous house, we liked the extra space. After the last one left, we found the extra space just meant extra rooms to clean and heat."

For the couple, this home is also about quality vs. quantity. They used natural and recycled materials wherever possible, and they say they enjoy their home so much, it doesn't feel like they traded down. "If anything," Carol says, "it feels more luxurious with all the glass, high ceiling wood beams, and modern architectural design features." And, according to Carol, their new 1,440-sq.-ft. home actually feels much more spacious than their previous 2,500-sq.-ft. home. Carol says that she is "happy to be simplifying and no longer accumulating. It's time, and it feels better."

Larry particularly enjoys the views from the house. "Because our bedroom has huge frosted-glass sliding doors we can choose to leave open, we can watch the stars and the moon move across the sky at night, we can watch the sunrise in the morning, and we have a magnificent view of all the wildlife during the day."

ABOVE: In the living room, a large wall of windows lets in ample natural light and offers a great view of the meadow outside. High ceilings provide a feeling of spaciousness, while the open floor plan minimizes wasted space and allows plenty of room to maneuver around furniture. Window seats on either side of the gas fireplace add extra seating when Larry and Carol have company.

RIGHT: The kitchen opens onto the living and dining areas as the core of the open floor plan. Generous floor space between the large central island and cabinets means that two or more people can prepare food at the same time, and that space allows maneuvering room for visitors with mobility issues. Heavy timber beams overhead add security and warmth to the interior.

From the front, the house looks like a small, modern but modest one-story home. The simple entrance opens onto a spacious, beautifully appointed interior with vaulted wood ceilings and a dramatic back wall of floor-to-ceiling windows with park-like views of the meadow and wetlands. The siding is cedar with corrugated metal highlights.

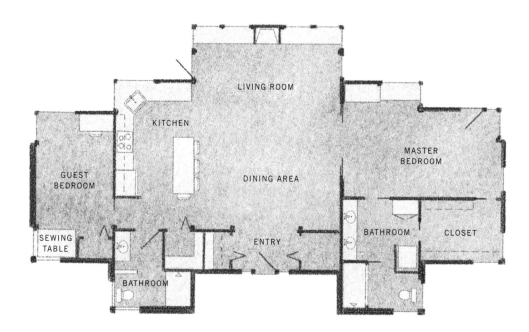

GREEN FEATURES
- Recycled metal roof
- Rainscreen behind siding
- Engineered bamboo flooring
- Recycled material in the countertops
- Dual-flush toilet
- Low-flow faucets and showers
- No-VOC paints
- Low-VOC caulks
- Whole-house fan

ENERGY-EFFICIENT FEATURES
- Deep overhangs
- Ductless heat pump
- LED and CFL lighting
- ENERGY STAR–rated appliances
- ENERGY STAR–rated ceiling fans

In the light-filled bedroom, carpet tiles are made of recycled materials. The tiles can be replaced one at a time as needed, so if one gets stained, it can be removed without tearing up and wasting the entire carpet.

The threshold-free shower and spacious bathroom layout offer easy maneuverability, if necessary in the future. A simple shower curtain is used so there are no shower doors as obstacles or hazards.

UNIVERSAL DESIGN

Universal design is the creation of space and products that all people at every stage in life and ability can use, a concept originally conceived for creating easier access for disabled people and now used to benefit a wider spectrum, including those with age-diminished physical capacity. According to UniversalDesign.com, "Everyone, even the most able-bodied person, passes through childhood, periods of temporary illness, injury, and old age. By designing for this human diversity, we can create things that will be easier for all people to use."

Selwyn Goldsmith pioneered the concept in his 1963 work, *Designing for the Disabled*. One of his achievements was the creation of dropped curbs, now standard in the built environment. Ronald Mace coined the term *universal design* in 1991.

As the U.S. population ages, universal design grows more important, and designers and engineers are developing new compliant products each year. Out of this concept evolved many now-common universal design features in homes, such as grab bars in showers and adequate task lighting. Several such features were incorporated into the Whidbey Island House, including the threshold-free shower and entry, wide doorways, a drawer dishwasher (which can be easily accessed by someone who is impaired), and handles on cupboards (which can be used by those with limited dexterity) instead of knobs. In addition the outside doors have lever handles for easy access.

FORD HOUSE

Modular

PHOTOGRAPHER
Allison Cartwright

ARCHITECT/BUILDER
Chris Krager
KRDB/MA

MANUFACTURER
Palm Harbor Homes

LOCATION
Austin, Texas

SIZE
1,500 sq. ft.

AFTER SEEING A HOUSE IN EAST AUSTIN THAT architect Chris Krager had designed and built, Karen and Joe hired him to design and build their own house on an infill lot they bought in the city's center. They already knew they wanted to build modular because of the savings it brings in both time and materials. They contacted Chris about building one of the designs from his firm's *ma* division.

Karen was excited about the idea of trying something new in construction, while Joe appreciated how quickly their house would be completed. Their friends' new homes or renovations all took more than a year, so they were particularly pleased to move in only three months after prefab work began in the factory.

MA DIVISION

Chris started the *ma* division as an offshoot of his design/build company KRDB, with the goal to make modern modular design more accessible and more affordable (previously, he had been designing and building more expensive custom homes). His concept for *ma* is to build energy-efficient prefabricated houses at a modest price, fully equipped with plumbing, electrical fixtures, and appliances. *Ma* is a Japanese term referring to the space between things or a pause in a phrase or music. Coincidentally, as an acronym *ma* also can stand for "modern affordable" and "modern architecture."

UPGRADING A MODEL HOME

Chris offers several *ma* floor plans that come with optional upgrades. For their house, Karen and Joe chose to enlarge two of the bedrooms by shrinking the middle bathrooms and eliminating a window. They also added 700 sq. ft. to the deck. They chose burnished stucco on the exterior, an optional upgrade from LaHabra®. This stucco has color incorporated into the finish coat, which is troweled or burnished to a smooth texture, a bit like a Venetian plaster finish. (Most other stucco has a textured or sand finish and is painted

For the siding, they upgraded to long-lasting massaranduba wood because it has no knots, is very dense, and minimizes insect damage and water absorption. Chris recommends massaranduba because "it's a beautiful, rot-resistant wood that is sustainably harvested in Brazil and is not insanely expensive." According to Joe, making these changes to the base model took about 30 seconds of consultation.

The only glitch in the whole process was the foundation, which had to be reengineered when soil testing failed to hit bedrock as anticipated. The

The siding on this house located on an infill lot is long-wearing, rot-resistant massaranduba (Brazilian hardwood) and burnished stucco. Xeriscaping minimizes the need for irrigation.

The wall of sliding glass doors and windows, topped by a band of clerestories, allows plenty of light into the open floor plan. The doors open onto an expansive deck.

XERISCAPING

The landscaping around the Ford House uses native plants, which minimizes the need for irrigation, fertilization, and pesticides. This is a type of landscaping known as xeriscaping. Drought-tolerant plants can thrive without a great deal of maintenance. As an extra benefit, they often flourish without pesticides and fertilizers, which could get into the water system. Besides enhancing the appearance of the house, native plants reduce runoff, save water, and reduce pollution that would have been created by lawn mowing. For further information on xeriscaping, visit the PlantNative website (plantnative.com).

The connector separates the two wings to create the courtyard and also serves as an extra room and foyer, which makes the overall space feel more generous than its 1,500 sq. ft.

house is in an area of Austin just west of the Balcones Escarpment, or fault zone, and the limestone substrata are uneven and unpredictable. The lot is over a void in the limestone, which is filled with clay soils. Because of the expansiveness of the soil fill, they had to forgo the shallow-set foundation, instead adding twenty-two 2-ft.-wide 15-ft.-deep piers, which tripled foundation costs.

It took 10 days to construct the modules in the factory, followed by a day to set the house on the foundation and eight weeks to complete the balance of the hookups and detail work. (It would have been only six weeks but for the rain delay that stalled the stucco contractor and driveway pour.)

SAVING ON ENERGY
Because of their home's excellent sealing and insulation, the couple's utility bills are much lower than other houses in the area. They pay about $225 a month in the summer but only about $100 a month

in the winter. The house has an electric heat pump for heating and air-conditioning. As Joe comments, "Given that we have regular hundred-degree days in the summer (which really lasts four or more months) and the house has fairly extensive glazing, $225 is very good." They chose an on-demand tankless water heater (see p. 107), which they recommend because they never run out of hot water and don't pay to continually heat a tank of water when not needed.

The layout of the house is also very efficient, with little space wasted to circulation—hallways, stairs, and corridors. This space saving, in conjunction with the courtyard layout and carefully placed and generous glazing, makes the house feel much larger than its 1,500 sq. ft.

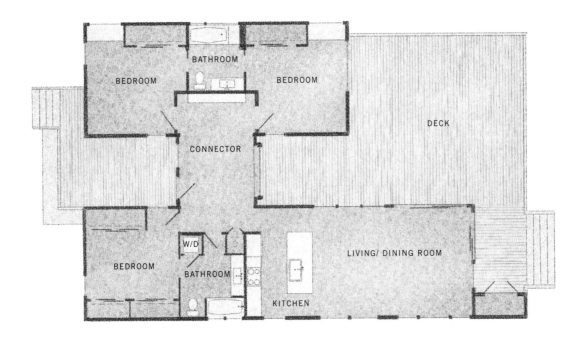

The proximity of the deck to the living area allows the parents to keep an eye on their children while they are cooking inside or relaxing in the living room.

GREEN FEATURES
- Bamboo flooring
- Low-flow toilets
- Low-flow faucets and showers
- Low- or no-VOC finishes
- Recycled materials
- Xeriscaping (see p. 104)

ENERGY-EFFICIENT FEATURES
- High-efficiency windows
- Large overhangs
- Radiant floor heating
- Tankless water heater
- ENERGY STAR–rated heat pump
- ENERGY STAR–rated appliances
- ENERGY STAR–rated ceiling fans

The H-shaped plan creates a breezeway for the house in the front and back. The house was fabricated in three sections: the large living/dining/kitchen with a bedroom and bath on one side, two bedrooms with a shared bath on the other side, and the connector/foyer in the center.

TANKLESS WATER HEATERS

A typical storage-tank water heater keeps water warm 24/7, wasting a huge amount of energy. With no storage tank, a tankless water heater (also known as a demand-type or instantaneous water heater) heats water only on the way to the faucet. Cold water circulates through a series of coils heated by either electric or gas heat. The heating element turns on only when a hot water faucet opens. With no tank to refill, water can be continuously heated, providing a constant flow of hot water.

Electric units provide hot water at a rate of 2 gal. to 5 gal. per minute, depending on the model. Gas-fired units produce higher flow rates than electric ones, although the pilot light, if left on continuously, wastes energy. Also, more than one tankless unit may be required to provide enough hot water for a family.

Tankless units generally cost more than a typical 40-gal. water heater but usually have longer warranties, last longer, and use less energy, saving money over the life of the tank. A storage-type water heater lasts between 10 years and 15 years, whereas a tankless heater can last more than 20 years. ENERGY STAR estimates that a typical family saves $100 or more per year with an ENERGY STAR–qualified tankless water heater. For more information, see the U.S. Department of Energy's website (eere.energy.gov); the tankless water heater used in this house is from Rinnai® (rinnai.us).

SONOMA RESIDENCE

Modular/Steel Frame

PHOTOGRAPHERS
Joe Fletcher (except
where noted)

ARCHITECT
Jared Levy/Gordon Stott
Connect Homes

MANUFACTURER
Connect Homes

INTERIOR DESIGNER
Meredith Rebolledo

LOCATION
Sonoma, Calif.

SIZE
1,600 sq. ft.

BUILDING A HOUSE FOR A PARENT PRESENTS challenges. Creating a house that is suitable for an aging person and convincing her to change her lifestyle are among the biggest ones. Carrie Kramlich took on this challenge and decided to build the house as a pre-fab, so she could control and expedite the construction.

BUILDING FOR MOM

Carrie's mom had been living by herself in downtown Sonoma but Carrie wanted to have her closer by, so she decided to build her mother a house on a lot adjoining her own. Carrie took a unique approach to building the home and made a careful plan to slowly convince her mother to make the move. Architects Jared Levy and Gordon Stott worked with Carrie on the design of the house to make it both beautiful and accommodating for an older person. The plan worked out well because Carrie understood how her mom lives and had a clear vision of what she needed.

Accommodations for her mom's needs included minimizing steps, installing a walk-in bathtub, and choosing appliances that are easily accessible, such as a drawer dishwasher and drawer microwave—all universal design features (see "Universal Design" on p. 101).

"We really enjoyed the process of working with Carrie at this level of detail for her mom," Jared said. Taking the lead, Carrie spared her mother from the detailed decisions that come with building a house, which gave her mom time to slowly adjust to the move. By the time the house was complete, Carrie's mom was fully on board with the move and excited about her new home.

MODULES DELIVERED ALMOST COMPLETE

It took about two months in the factory to build the Sonoma residence. Unlike some modular companies, Connect Homes modules are 95% complete when they leave the factory. As a result, they require less on-site finishing than some other modular houses on the market. Doors, windows, interior and exterior finishes, plumbing, mechanical, and electrical systems are all finished in the factory. Only "marriage" lines (which seam module to module) and basic utility hookups are done on site.

It took only weeks, not months to complete the house on site. Less on-site finishing means fewer variables that can go wrong—and there's less waste and less environmental strain put on the site with trucks coming and going onto the property. This activity often requires cutting down trees to make room for deliveries and materials storage but that was not necessary here.

To take advantage of the beautiful surroundings, the house was designed with large sliding doors aligning front and back to open up stunning see-through views of the Sonoma Valley. Exterior siding is western red cedar with black metal trim.

Flooring throughout the house is FSC-certified sustainably harvested bamboo. Furnishings are a mix of items sourced from a local vintage furniture store and some things the owner brought with her. Track lights all use LED fixtures.

While the modules were built in the factory, the owner did all predelivery site work, such as preparing the foundation and clearing the site, preserving as many of the trees as possible. The house was then completed about six weeks after it was delivered. The private road leading up to the site, though beautiful with amazing groves of trees and views, did have some intense grades and hairpin turns. Architect Jared admits that there were a few anxious moments watching the trucks go up the road, but they all got there.

AGING IN PLACE

Carrie is delighted with the finished house. She says that at this time in her mother's life, "she's living in a home that is bursting with light and sunshine. She is surrounded by nature and connecting with it on a deeper level than she has ever done in her eighty-nine years. I don't see how it gets better than that."

Since her mother moved into the house, Carrie reports that she's become less mobile, but because Carrie planned ahead and the architects understood "aging in place" as a design concept, it has been a seamless transition. When her mother needed a wheelchair after returning from a hospital stay, it was easy. There were no stairs, no carpeting, no thresholds—but there was easy access to the bathroom and the kitchen. After her recovery, she used a walker for a time, and again, the transition process was seamless.

While the house accommodates her mother's infirmities, it doesn't feel like a home for the infirm or incapacitated. According to Carrie, "The house is so graceful and the design so inviting, it's a beautiful, contemporary home for anyone, at any age. Maybe that's the best way to describe aging in place. You need never leave the house you've created, that you've worked to make into a home. Timeless, sensible design works for a thirty-year-old and is just as great when that thirty-year-old is lucky enough to see ninety."

The large sliding doors in the dining area provide natural lighting, ventilation, and inspiring views. Because the owner built the house with her mom's accessibility issues in mind, decks are flush with the landscape in back, which also serves to more completely connect the house to the site.

GLASS WOOL INSULATION

Glass wool insulation is made from glass fibers, sand, and a binder that combines the two into a material that possesses a texture similar to wool. The process traps many small pockets of air between the glass fibers. The air in turn prevents the transfer of heat and produces the thermal insulation properties of the material.

To make the insulation, recycled glass and sand are heated to 2,642°F (1,450°C) and forced through a fine mesh using high-speed spinners to form fibers, which have a wool-like texture. (This process is similar to the way cotton candy is made.) Next, binders are added that cement the fibers together, and then the fibers, now formed into mats, are heated once more. Glass wool is light; offers good acoustic and thermal insulation; and is available in rolls, panels, or loose for blown-in insulation.

EcoBatt® Insulation, used for the Sonoma Residence, contains no phenol, formaldehyde, acrylics, or artificial colors; uses recycled glass; and is GREENGUARD certified (see p. 115). The company claims to use 70% less embodied energy in their binders than traditional petroleum-based binders. For additional information about the insulation used in this house, visit EcoBatt's website (ecobatt.us).

ABOVE: Wide sliding doors open the bedroom to the outside and to an inviting small deck where the owner can sit and be surrounded by natural beauty.

FACING PAGE LEFT: The kitchen is in the center of the home's public space and includes a large island that can be used for food prep, serving, seating, and eating. Because this house was built for the owner's mother, who doesn't do a great deal of cooking, appliances are compact.

FACING PAGE RIGHT: The tiles that cover the walls of the bathroom are made from recycled glass and postconsumer recycled content.

Photo courtesy of Connect Homes

RECYCLED-GLASS COUNTERTOPS

Recycled-glass countertops incorporate mostly recycled glass with either cement or resin binders. The finished product is very strong, easy to clean, and nontoxic. The product comes in a variety of colors and is resistant to moisture, heat, chemicals, and mold. Cement versions must be sealed when installed and again every one to five years, when water no longer beads on the surface. The recycled glass countertop used in the Sonoma Residence is made by IceStone®. For additional information about this product, visit the manufacturer's website (icestoneusa.com).

TOP: The steel frame under construction in the factory.

BOTTOM: The module is carried on a flatbed truck to the site where it will be set.

Photos courtesy of Connect Homes

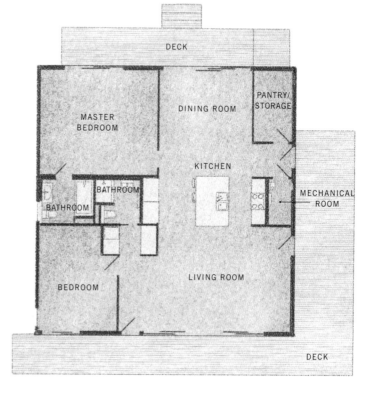

GREEN FEATURES
- Recycled steel frame
- Sustainably harvested western red cedar siding
- FSC-certified bamboo flooring
- Cradle to Cradle Certified™ recycled glass/cement countertops (gold level)
- Recycled glass tile
- Dual-flush/low-flow toilets
- Low-flow faucets and showers
- Low- or no-VOC finishes, paints, adhesives, and primers

ENERGY-EFFICIENT FEATURES
- Cool roof system
- Energy-efficient windows and doors
- High-efficiency glass doors
- High-efficiency tankless water heater
- GREENGUARD-certified glass wool insulation
- LED and CFL lighting
- ENERGY STAR–rated appliances
- Convection cooktop

Breathtaking views of the valley below make the deck a magical spot to relax, daydream, or host an intimate dinner or cocktail party. It's also a great place to watch the sun set over the Sonoma Valley.

GREENGUARD CERTIFICATION PROGRAM

The GREENGUARD certification program, administered by UL Environment, assures homeowners, builders, and specifiers that certified products designed for use in indoor spaces meet strict chemical emissions limits, contributing to the creation of healthier interiors. GREENGUARD certification gives credibility to manufacturers' sustainability claims, backed by scientific data attained by an unbiased, third-party organization. Product categories certified in the program include building materials, flooring, finishes, paints and sealants, interior furnishings, cabinetry, cleaning products, and electronic equipment. For additional information about this certification program, visit the UL website (ul.com/gg), where you'll also find a searchable list of sustainable products.

COUSINS
RIVER RESIDENCE

SIPs

PHOTOGRAPHER
Trent Bell

ARCHITECT/BUILDER/
INTERIOR DESIGN
GO Logic

BLOWER DOOR TEST
0.6 ACH50

LOCATION
Freeport, Maine

SIZE
1,600 sq. ft.

ELLEN AND NICHOLAS WALSH DECIDED TO DOWN-size by about half the space they had been occupying and built their empty-nest house in Freeport, along Maine's southern coast. It sits on the bluff of Cousins River, one of several local estuaries that flow into the Atlantic. They built it for themselves, but with room for their three college-age children when they return in the summer and during school breaks.

DOWNSIZING AS EMPTY NESTERS

The couple's previous home was a 3,000-sq.-ft. Sears kit house built in 1908 that cost $5,000 a year to heat. "We loved the house," says Ellen, "but it was admittedly a bit poky and hard to clean and maintain." When the house sold quickly, they took an apartment in the local village for a year while they built their current home.

As part of the downsizing process, they had to sell off lots of accessories and other possessions. Scaling back was a mostly "painless" process with a few exceptions. "It's the first cut that is the most difficult," both agree. Ellen's family has been in New Haven for 300 years, and she had some beautiful old furniture, such as a highboy, chest, and tables. "One or two pieces made it into the new house, where we think they work, some were sold, and a few are in storage for our kids," she said.

The new house is perfect for the two of them. "We love the design, the light, the constant fresh air provided by the air exchanger, the view, and just about everything else about it," she said. When their kids are home, the three bedrooms are full but the house remains comfortable and easy. "It is not a house that suffers clutter, and we are somewhat insistent on keeping the living areas clear."

BUILDING TO PASSIVHAUS STANDARDS

Ellen and Nicholas approached GO Logic because the firm specializes in designing and building Passivhaus homes. The owners also wanted a low-maintenance, highly efficient home with a clean and contemporary aesthetic.

Go Logic designed this house to Passivhaus (see the Glossary on p. 222) international energy-efficiency standards, although Ellen and Nicholas decided not to apply for certification. Using those standards, their home's reliance on electric energy to heat and cool is reduced as much as 90% from traditional building standards.

To achieve such efficiency, the design had to be especially responsive to the cold Maine winters. During winter, light and heat from the low

Although the shape of the house is modern, it was inspired by the basic country shed roof. The low horizontal lines of the single-level home contrast nicely with the trees that surround it. This southern side of the house is mostly the public side, with the kitchen and living room, and includes the master bedroom (at right). Siding is painted fiber cement clapboard beneath a standing-seam metal roof.

In the living room, large expanses of glass and a high cathedral ceiling create a generous sense of space for the home's small footprint. Crafted of clear-finished Baltic birch plywood with mill-finished steel dividers, the bookcase has integrated lighting in the display shelf. Its acid-etched glass is backlit from the hallway at night.

ABOVE: The kitchen cabinets were custom made from hard and durable ash wood and painted with a high-gloss latex enamel paint. Countertops are local Maine granite, while the concrete floor has a smooth, power-troweled finish with a matte sealer. A dye was used to change the color of the floor from gray to a subtle limestone.

LEFT: The custom-designed bookcase not only provides needed storage but also acts as a buffer between the guest bedrooms/ guest bath and the main living space. It simultaneously connects the master bedroom suite to the kitchen/entry without leading through the main space.

The door from the master bedroom onto the front deck is tilt and turn so it can allow air in without being totally opened. The custom cabinetry is ash.

southern sun are let in through well-sited windows and are kept in by ultra-thick walls, minimal thermal bridging, and triple-glazed windows. The windows (R-8) boast a 50% solar heat gain. Concrete floors provide a substantial thermal mass, helping maintain the heat. In the summer when the sun is high in the sky, the overhangs block the sun.

Because the house, like all Passivhauses, was built extremely tight, it required an HRV to keep the air fresh in the house without losing heated or cooled air. Energy loss is minimized with an extremely efficient thermal envelope (see "The Thermal Envelope" on p. 122). The foundation (R-70) is a patented superinsulated system, and the R-50 panelized walls are built with a double-wall system. The inner wall is made with densely packed cellulose insulation and the outer wall with SIPs and rigid expanded polystyrene (EPS) foam. The roof (R-80) system is also superinsulated.

Combined with the high performance of the house envelope, a small PV array (4.6 kilowatts) on the roof provides electricity. The home generates about as much energy as it uses, making it near net-zero.

HEATING AND COOLING

The open floor plan is oriented to solar south, with vaulted interior spaces under the shed roof, which projects over the south facade to shade the house in the summer. Heating is primarily provided by passive solar methods, with supplemental back-up from electric baseboard heaters zoned from room to room on individual thermostats. In cooler weather, the house stays warm without additional heating because of the excellent insulation and the highly efficient German windows and doors. A small wood stove, which burns Envi Blocks or BioBricks®, is put to use most nights between mid-December and mid-February, saving a great deal on energy costs.

There is no mechanical cooling system. In the summer, Ellen and Nicholas open windows and doors at night to let the house cool down. When the sun comes up in the morning, they close the doors and windows. Even if it is hot outside, the house remains about 10° cooler than the outside.

SAVING ON UTILITIES

Sustainability has been a recurring theme in Ellen's career as a teacher. Now she loves living in a house that makes most of its own electricity and that otherwise has a small impact on the planet.

With the PV panels providing more energy than they use, Ellen and Nicholas are able to sell excess electricity back to the grid. According to Ellen, "In our first twelve months our total net energy costs, excluding a half-cord equivalent of BioBricks for the stove, were about $550, which is pretty spectacular. A more traditional home of this size, with electric heat, would probably cost about $4,000 for the same period, and it wouldn't be nearly as comfortable."

The master bathroom includes a soaking tub and shower with hand-cut fossilized tile (with actual fossils). The glass partition has a fused coating that seals the surface with a protective barrier that keeps it clear and resists corrosion.

THE THERMAL ENVELOPE

The envelope or shell of a house must be structurally sound and protect the house from the elements—wind, water, weather, and sun. The envelope includes the foundation, walls, windows/doors, and roof. This exterior armor is the most important factor in maintaining heating and cooling in the house and preventing mold and mildew.

The materials for the envelope must be climate appropriate, structurally sound, and aesthetically pleasing. Working together, the various parts of the envelope must stop or slow the flow of air, water, and heat, while still allowing a way for water that gets in to dry out.

Air leaks in a house's envelope can be found during construction by using a blower door test (see the Glossary on p. 222), which can expose areas of air infiltration. Leaks can then be sealed with tape, spray foam, rubber gaskets, and caulking. For additional information, see the National Renewable Energy Laboratory's website (nrel.gov).

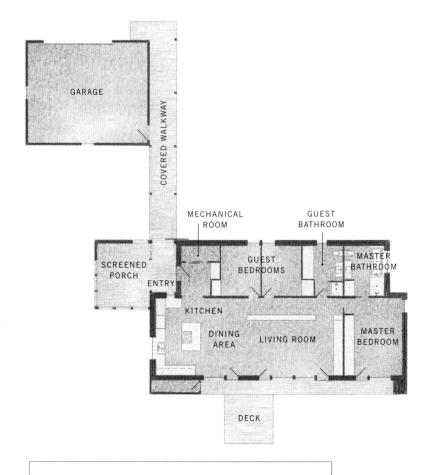

GREEN FEATURES
- Dual-flush toilets
- Low-flow faucets and showers
- Low- or no-VOC finishes
- Locally sourced materials

ENERGY-EFFICIENT FEATURES
- PV panels
- Triple-pane windows
- Large overhangs
- HRV
- Concrete floors
- High-efficiency wall system
- LED and CFL lighting
- ENERGY STAR–rated appliances

A covered walkway leads to the garage from the northern facade of the house, which is the private side and the location of two smaller bedrooms, two bathrooms, and the mudroom entry.

ABOVE: The grade-level deck off the living room is a favorite spot where the owners can enjoy beautiful Maine mornings or an outdoor meal.

LEFT: The screened porch can be used for three seasons (it is in Maine, after all). Its flooring is Port Orford cedar, a particularly hard, strong, and decay-resistant wood. Exterior paneling is locally milled pine. The screen door can be closed off at the walkway, and the entry door to the house left open so the interior space flows seamlessly to the exterior.

WEEZERO HOUSE

Modular

PHOTOGRAPHY
Courtesy of Alchemy
Architects

ARCHITECT
Geoffrey Warner
Alchemy Architects

MANUFACTURER
Irontown Homes

BUILDER
Foundation/site work
by owner

LOCATION
Moab, Utah

SIZE
1,625 sq. ft.

THIS UTAH VACATION HOME WAS BUILT FOR A family that lives in a Minneapolis suburb. Moab is an ideal escape from the rigorous Minneapolis winter, a place where the owners can enjoy the beauty of the nearby national park, mountain bike, ski, and hike, depending on the season.

BUILDING A ZERO-ENERGY HOME

Utah is a perfect location for building a zero-energy house. The state gets ample sun and enjoys relatively warm daytime temperatures year round. Orienting the house to the south allows passive heat gain through the glass and creates a logical plane to mount solar thermal panels. With active solar thermal panels and passive solar design, including passive solar orientation, daylighting, and minimal glazing at the western exposure, heating requirements are kept to a minimum.

The owners eventually intend to move to Moab full time, at which point they'll invest in PV panels. The solar power will offset the cooling and other domestic energy costs they now incur. Even when PV panels are installed, the house will still be tied to the grid because otherwise storage-cell batteries would be needed, which require periodic replacement.

THE WEEHOUSE CONCEPT

Alchemy Architects are known internationally for their design of the wee-House®, a modular prefabricated housing system that optimizes many elements of the traditional design–build process. Their original weeHouse was built in Pepin, Wisconsin, in 2003 and was a simple 350-sq.-ft. retreat the company owners built themselves on a $50,000 budget. Built just before the explosion in media attention for prefab and tiny houses, the house received a lot of notice for its spatial modesty, off-site prefabrication, and strong connections to the landscape.

To leverage the work and thinking that went into that house, architect Geoffrey Warner and his Alchemy team broke the house down into a series of prefabricated boxes as sleeping, bathing, or living units that could be recombined to form both small and large houses. "Building is difficult, time-consuming, and expensive," Geoffrey says. "People are attracted to solutions that can reduce those impacts, while still retaining the flexibility for the process to adapt to them personally. A range of finishes and products allows us and our clients to more quickly get to a design, a cost, and a timeline that they feel is worth pursuing."

The area where this house is located is sparsely populated, with houses barely visible to one another between the red rock desert formations. The simple box appears to hover over the landscape.

GOING FOR PREFABRICATION

The owners of the weeZero house thought that Alchemy was the right company to build their vacation home. Given its remote location and the relative scarcity and cost of qualified local labor, the house was a good candidate for prefabrication. The architect's initial design consultation with the owners took a few weeks; working drawings and factory planning took about six months, and construction in the factory another two months.

The house was delivered with everything but the furniture. After the foundation was installed and the house was set, the roofing, siding, and systems rough-ins were completed in a week. Finishing materials were installed at the seams between modules, and the owners completed all finishes such as flooring, tile, and gypsum board installation in a few short visits.

WATER COLLECTION AND HEATING

Water is a precious resource in Utah, and in Moab it comes mainly from a few major rain events. A water tank was installed in the basement before the house was set. Gutters and a gray water system will be added when the house is converted to full-time use.

FACING PAGE TOP: The kitchen has highly durable quartz countertops and stock IKEA cabinets. Bamboo flooring carries up the face of the island in a color similar to the cabinets, giving all a custom look. A pullout hood is tucked inside the horizontal upper cabinet, leaving open storage above.

FACING PAGE BOTTOM: The bedroom design is treated with the playfulness of a boat berth, which creates some separation and privacy despite tight quarters. (Another bed is in a corner of the room, not visible in the photo.) The ceiling fan cools effectively in the evening without air-conditioning when the landscape cools. The heat pump can be seen on the wall to the left.

Solar hot water panels on the roof and a heat-exchange tank provide the in-floor hydronic heat, widely considered to be the most comfortable type of home heating. High-efficiency multi-split wall units provide cooling as well as backup heat, if necessary.

LESS IS MORE

According to Geoffrey, the house "is an exercise in restraint and a less-is-more approach on many levels in context with the landscape, material simplicity, and budget." The owners originally wanted a three-bedroom house, but concessions on scale and size led to combining sleeping needs into a second bedroom with open beds and an alcove, which makes the house more interesting, cozy, and sustainable (and less expensive).

COR-TEN STEEL

Cor-Ten steel is a weathering-type steel. It combines alloys meant to develop a rust exterior that acts as a protective coating if the material is left untreated and exposed to the elements. Weathering steel exhibits increased resistance to atmospheric corrosion compared to other types of steel and eliminates the need for painting and rust-prevention maintenance. Cor-Ten's protective surface layer, or patina, protects it from further corrosion.

Humid subtropical climates and water pooling on the steel may destabilize the coating, however, leading to corrosion. Weathering steel is best used in a dry environment and on a structure with adequate drainage. Cor-Ten is manufactured by U.S. Steel®.

With the first module already set onto the precast concrete foundation, the adjoining module is lowered by crane to mate up with the first. The Cor-Ten steel siding covers both sections, but because the house was factory-made, the steel has not yet oxidized.

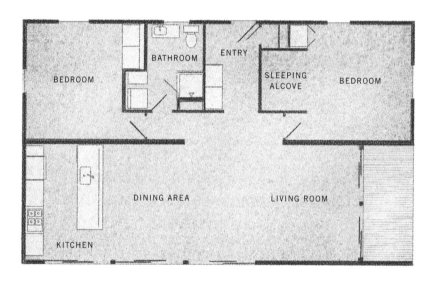

BEDROOM

BATHROOM

ENTRY

SLEEPING ALCOVE

BEDROOM

DINING AREA

LIVING ROOM

KITCHEN

GREEN FEATURES

• Flexible space
• Metal siding
• No carpeting
• Bamboo flooring
• Low-flow faucets and showerheads
• Dual-flush toilets
• Zero-VOC paint
• Xeriscaping

ENERGY-EFFICIENT FEATURES

• Passive solar orientation
• Solar thermal panels
• Daylighting
• Minimal glazing at western exposure
• Cross ventilation
• High-efficiency heat pump
• Mini-split system
• Hydronic radiant heating
• CFL lighting
• ENERGY STAR–rated appliances
• Prewired for PV panels

The solar thermal panels on the roof are covered, as mandated by local guidelines.

MODERN HEAT PUMP MINI- AND MULTI-SPLIT SYSTEMS

A great deal of confusion exists about heat pumps and the terminology used to describe them, which is unfortunate because they are a terrific way to save energy and reduce the cost of heating and cooling. These units are much more popular outside the United States, where energy is more expensive and there is a greater concern for conservation.

Heat pump mini- and multi-split systems are composed of an outside compressor/condenser unit and one or several air handlers inside the house. If there is one inside unit and one outside unit, the system is called a split or mini-split system. If there is one outside unit and multiple inside units (up to eight), it is called a multi-split system. Multi-split systems can be ducted, and the air-handler units can be behind a wall. However, the units can also be ductless and mounted on the wall or suspended from or mounted flush with the ceiling. Ductless systems avoid the loss of energy that is often associated with ducted systems and take up less space inside the house. They can also be installed more easily in retrofits than other types of heating and cooling systems.

The number of units a home requires depends on the efficiency of its thermal envelope. If the house has been built airtight with excellent insulation, less heat and air-conditioning will be required and consequently fewer heat pump units.

The source for heating and cooling with mini- and multi-split heat pump systems comes from the air (called *air-to-air units*), from water (*air-to-water units*), or from the ground (*air-to-ground geothermal units*).

LG, the company that supplied the unit for the weeZero House, offers an attractive alternative to the traditional air handler typically seen in homes and commercial properties. These units are covered by 24-in. by 24-in. frames that can hold art prints or mirrors to camouflage the air handler. The interior units can be purchased in a variety of different air-handler styles, each controlled by its own remote control.

For best results, consumers should look for an ENERGY STAR–compliant unit. For additional information about these units, visit the U.S. Department of Energy's website (energy.gov/energysaver/articles/ductless-mini-split-heat-pumps) or the LG website (lghomecomfort.com)

CLOVERDALE HOUSE

Modular

PHOTOGRAPHER
Jaime Kowal

ARCHITECT
Chris Pardo, Design
Elemental Architecture

MANUFACTURER/
BUILDER
Method Homes

LOCATION
Cloverdale, Calif.

SIZE
1,670 sq. ft.

WHEN JANET AND ROY DECIDED THAT THEY WANTED a modular house, they went online to look for manufacturers. They came across the Method Homes website and found a floor plan exactly like what they were looking for. After connecting with Method Homes, they decided to build that house. Janet likes to joke that they bought their house on the Internet.

WHY MODULAR

The homeowners admired the modular houses they'd seen in *Dwell*® magazine over the years. "They were incredibly efficient, interesting uses of new (to us) materials and great design without having to start from scratch," Roy said. "After having always lived in older homes, we wanted something modern, and modular seemed the best way to go about it." Janet and Roy appreciated the quality material choices Method Homes offered, which helped them narrow the available options.

As avid cyclists, Janet and Roy were attracted to Cloverdale, a location that has great areas for riding. They also liked the beautiful landscape and local weather. After living in the San Francisco fog for 30 years, they decided they needed some sun for their next adventure.

The couple was ready to downsize from a much larger house, a move that they said was very "liberating." Unfortunately, their old style of furniture didn't work well in the new house, so they replaced most of it with the help of Craigslist® and eBay®.

CONSTRUCTION WAS QUICK

Factory construction of the house took three months. Setting the house took a day, with the last unit going in just as the sun was setting. Although the steep hill and tight turns in the road to the site proved difficult for the truck driver, by the end of the day the house was weathertight (dried in). It took another two months to complete all electrical and plumbing hook-ups and interior and exterior details. Five months after they purchased the house, Janet and Roy moved in.

HEATING AND COOLING

Because the house is so well insulated, heating and cooling are kept to a minimum. The house is heated with four mini-split heat pumps, which also provide air-conditioning. Cloverdale's climate gets hot but usually cools off in the evening, often with a 40° difference between a day's high and low temperatures. According to Janet, "The mini-splits seem perfect for those kinds of conditions."

The cantilevered portion of the house provides a covered area for the outdoor living space below. The roof deck off the kitchen on the upper level offers beautiful vineyard views.

BLOWN-IN FIBERGLASS INSULATION

Nearly everyone's familiar with blown-in foam insulation, but blown-in fiberglass is also an option. Blowing in insulation fills gaps in the wall and gets into areas that are difficult to fill with preformed batts. However, unlike foam, fiberglass is blown in dry so walls are immediately ready for sheathing.

Depending on the density of the installation, fiberglass offers excellent thermal efficiency and sound control. The insulation used in the Cloverdale House is OPTIMA® loose-fill. Fabric is stapled across the studs to enclose them, then holes are cut in the fabric and the loose fill is blown into the opening to completely fill it. The insulation can create an R-value of R-15 in 2×4 framing, up to R-23 in 2×6 framing, and R-56 in 2×14 framing. This product is formaldehyde-free and, according to the manufacturer, won't settle to leave gaps at the top. It is also GREENGUARD Gold certified (see "GREENGUARD Certification Program" on p. 115) for indoor air quality.

For more info on OPTIMA, visit the CertainTeed website (certainteed.com/insulation). Owens Corning® also manufactures a blown-in fiberglass insulation (owenscorning.com).

TOP: Kitchen appliances are ENERGY STAR rated, and the virtually indestructible stainless-steel backsplash is easily wiped clean. Countertops are a hand-cast, fibrous-cement material composed of recycled paper, recycled glass, and low-carbon cement. The narrow window behind the sink brings light into the cooking area and provides a view of the home's surroundings.

BOTTOM: A wonderful view of the vineyards and valley below provides a tempting respite from work in this home office. Recessed window shades lower to block out the afternoon sun. Floors are bamboo.

The monumental movie light between the living and dining area came from a store that sells oddities, home furnishings, and curiosities. The light supposedly was used on the movie *The Right Stuff*. Rather than blind their guests, the owners replaced the high-powered innards with a 60-watt bulb.

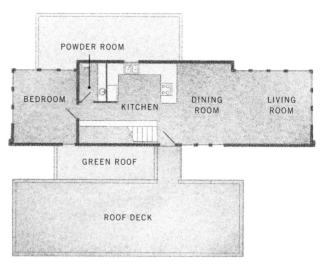

SECOND FLOOR

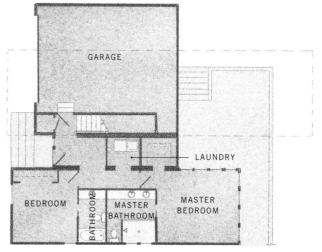

FIRST FLOOR

The lines, textures, and colors of the house perfectly complement the northern California landscape.

GREEN FEATURES
- Recycled metal siding
- FSC-certified bamboo flooring
- NAUF trim and doors
- Recycled content in concrete counters
- FSC-certified wood cabinetry
- Low-flow faucets and showers
- Dual-flush toilets
- Low- or no-VOC paints, finishes, and adhesives
- Drought-resistant landscape

ENERGY-EFFICIENT FEATURES
- ERV
- Heat pump hot water heater
- Ductless mini-split units for heating and cooling
- Blown-in fiberglass insulation (see p. 132)
- LED lighting
- ENERGY STAR–rated appliances
- ENERGY STAR–rated ceiling fans

The drought-resistant landscaping around the house requires no watering in the Mediterranean-like climate. Siding on the house is a combination of standing-seam metal, cedar cladding, and stucco. The garage doors are aluminum and glass, which give the house clean, modern lines.

SMART CEILING FANS

Ceiling fans don't actually cool air but move air, which helps evaporate perspiration which in turn cools the skin. These fans have always been an energy-saving method of making a room feel cooler, but they have recently become a lot more sophisticated.

Haiku® fans, the type of ceiling fan used in the Cloverdale house, are equipped with a computer (which the company calls SenseME™) and an array of sensors. This mechanism monitors environmental conditions, turns itself on when people enter the room and off when they leave, makes speed adjustments to keep the room comfortable, and programs itself to the homeowners' preferences. A smartphone app can schedule the fan to turn on and off at preferred times. An optional LED light can be programmed to go on in the morning for a gradual wake-up. The fan has a winter mode that pushes heat downward into the living space, reduces heating costs, and integrates with the Nest Learning Thermostat® (see "A Thermostat That Learns" on p. 187). The Haiku fan is ENERGY STAR rated. For additional information, visit the Big Ass Fans website (bigassfans.com/senseme).

SILICON VALLEY BALANCE HOUSE

Modular/SIPs/
Steel frame

PHOTOGRAPHER
John Swain

ARCHITECT
Claire Sheridan, director
of product development
Blu Homes®

MANUFACTURER/
BUILDER
Blu Homes

HERS INDEX
55

CERTIFICATIONS
CALGreen® (see p. 140)

LOCATION
Portola Valley, Calif.

SIZE
1,746 sq. ft.

UNIQUE TO MODULAR CONSTRUCTION, BLU HOMES builds houses that can be folded and more easily packed for travel from the factory to their destination. The Balance model, one of Blu Homes standard designs, was customized for this client by adding a lower level built on site along with the foundation while the upper level was constructed in the factory. The structure was then delivered and set atop the lower level and foundation. The house took about 6 weeks to build in the factory, just one day to set, and about 10 weeks to complete on site.

The home's current owner was initially looking to buy a fixer-upper, because he knew what features he wanted but didn't believe he'd find a completed house that would contain everything on his list. When a real estate agent showed him this house, he was surprised to find it had almost everything he was looking for.

PLACING THE MODULAR UNIT
The lower level was site built so it could be nestled tightly into the slope. It houses the garage, a bedroom, sitting room, and workshop. So many seismic, drainage, and structural issues had to be addressed on the lower level that the owner thought it made sense to solve those issues with a custom solution: site building the lower level and building the upper level using modular construction. Placing the modular units on top of the site-built lower level raised the house, walls, windows, and sliding doors to a height at which they provide beautiful views across the valley.

LIMITED ENERGY USE
The house has a condensing boiler (see p. 139), which is used to provide both domestic hot water and hot water for the floor hydronic radiant heating system. A special pump that distributes water throughout the house is a highly efficient way to heat because very little energy is lost in the process of heating water for both the radiant system and for washing and bathing.

To limit energy use, appliances and ceiling fans are ENERGY STAR rated and light bulbs are all CFLs. A roof of SIPs greatly increased the energy efficiency and interior comfort. Advanced framing was used to reduce thermal bridging in the exterior walls.

"This house, in its location, is in a completely different world," the homeowner claims. "Every day, I get to leave the concrete, asphalt, and cars and when I round the last corner of the road and the house comes into view, I know my 'vacation' has begun . . . at least until the alarm clock goes off the next day."

Proprietary cedar sliding doors on the Balance Home's front are aesthetically pleasing, allow indoor–outdoor living, and provide security and airflow. The outer sliding sunshades, which are made of clear cedar, allow the breeze to blow through while keeping sunshine out. The sliding doors can be left open while the sunshades are locked shut, to provide security and to let the outdoors in.

Clerestory windows introduce additional light in the high-ceilinged living area, and the ENERGY STAR–rated fan makes the room feel cooler. Flooring throughout is bamboo; the gas fireplace is direct vent (see the Glossary on p. 222).

TOP: Clerestory windows in the guest bedroom bring in extra light and cross ventilation.

BOTTOM: The toxin-free wood veneer kitchen cabinets are built from locally sourced cherry and are American made from a nearby supplier. The doors are high-efficiency sliders.

CONDENSING BOILERS

Condensing boilers have been popular for years in Europe and are now beginning to replace traditional boilers in the United States. A condensing boiler is a water heating system designed to recover energy that normally is discharged up the chimney as waste. That recovered energy is used to preheat cold water entering the boiler. Water vapor produced by the burning of gas in the boiler condenses into liquid and releases its latent heat. Unlike traditional boilers, a condensing boiler recovers the latent heat through vaporization using a heat exchanger.

The condensing boiler used in the Silicon Valley Balance House is by Viessman® and is ENERGY STAR rated. The company claims a 95% annual fuel utilization efficiency (AFUE) rating on its current models. According to the ENERGY STAR website (energystar.gov), AFUE is the percentage of the heat in the incoming fuel that is converted to space heat instead of being lost. For additional information on the unit used in this house, visit Viessman's website (viessmann-us.com).

CALGREEN

CALGreen is California's Green Building Code, which was first established in 2010 (and revised in 2013). It was founded to promote environmentally responsible, healthy, and cost-effective construction and to reduce water consumption. The code affects the planning and design of construction, energy, water, material conservation, and the environmental quality of the structure. CALGreen is mandatory in all state-owned buildings, all residential dwellings, and public schools. For further information, visit the California Building Standards Commission website (bsc.ca.gov/home/calgreen.aspx).

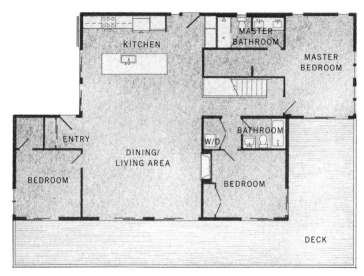

UPPER LEVEL

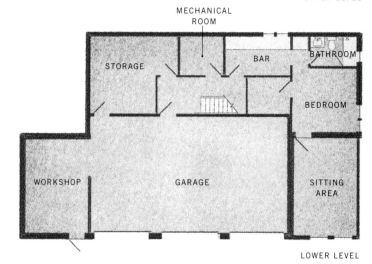

LOWER LEVEL

GREEN FEATURES
- Recycled-steel frame
- Bamboo flooring
- No carpeting
- Quartz countertops
- GREENGUARD-certified cabinetry
- Low-water appliances
- Low-flow faucets and showerheads
- Low-water toilets
- Low- or no-VOC finishes

ENERGY-EFFICIENT FEATURES
- Clerestory windows
- HRV
- Hydronic radiant heating
- High-efficiency water heater
- SIPs roof
- CFL lights
- ENERGY STAR–rated appliances
- ENERGY STAR–rated ceiling fans

The wraparound deck on the second level provides plenty of outdoor sitting space, and the garage doors with frosted glass panels add a modern touch. The steel cable rail fence—elegant, modern, and functional—was added as an upgrade.

HIGH-DEFINITION PRINTING ON PORCELAIN TILES

A new digital printing technique is being used to create a variety of designs on porcelain. The porcelain can be made to look like wood, rustic stone, marble, or slate and even close up is indistinguishable from the real thing. Printing is done with more than 500 injectors and multiple print heads so that a pattern is not repeated for 180 ft. This process creates tiles that are varied and have minimal repetition.

The glaze is sprayed on, rather than applied with a brush or some other method that comes into direct contact with the surface of the tile. Florida Tile®'s machinery recycles its own ink and produces no waste, creating a more efficient production line. Digital printing is also extremely low maintenance and incorporates an automated self-cleaning system. The company's HDP High Definition Porcelain® is a proprietary name and process. For more information, visit Florida Tile's website (floridatile.com/hdp-high-definition-porcelain).

The bathroom has a barrier-free shower with travertine wall tiles. Floor tiles are porcelain decorated using a high-definition technique in digital printing technology. The technique provides greater variety and less repetition, making the printed tiles indistinguishable from natural stone.

VASHON ISLAND HOUSE

Timber Frame/SIPs

PHOTOGRAPHERS
Dale Lang (except where noted)

ARCHITECT
FabCab

MANUFACTURER
FraserWood Industries (timber frame)

Premier Building Systems (SIPs)

BUILDER
Greg Kruse, Potential Energy

BLOWER DOOR TEST
2.69 ACH50

CERTIFICATIONS
Built Green™: 3 stars

LOCATION
Vashon Island, Wash.

SIZE
1,750 sq. ft.

JED AND SARA WANTED THEIR NEW BABY TO GROW up in a house surrounded by the beauty of nature. They purchased 9 acres in a secluded area of Washington's Vashon Island, both to get away from the stress of city life and to enjoy the beauty and tranquility of the island.

At first, they couldn't afford to build a house, so they pitched tents and spent more than a year camping on the property whenever they could get away for weekends and vacations. Eventually, they were ready to build their home where the tents were once located.

Their plan was for a cozy, compact cabin with a screened porch, which would create an experience of living with nature. The house was built on a slope and has a butterfly roof to catch light from both east and west. The large screened porch and deep roof overhangs provide plenty of space for indoor–outdoor living.

FINDING A WAY TO CUT COSTS

Jed and Sara started by commissioning an architect to design their house. However, after the home was permitted, construction costs came in at about twice their budget. The original design was much bigger, had more complicated detailing, and had more expensive materials than their Vashon Island House now has. It also had a good deal of concrete, all of which drove up the cost.

So, the couple asked FabCab to design them a different, more affordable house. Because the previous design was already permitted, FabCab architect Emory Baldwin had to work within the footprint of the previous design. Otherwise, he would have had to go through an extensive civil engineering review process because the house site was surrounded by a steep slope on three sides.

BUILDING WITH TIMBER FRAME AND SIPS

The structure of the house is a premilled timber frame on top of which are installed interlocking SIPs for rigidity and thermal resistance. According to builder Greg Kruse, this was a highly efficient process from design to construction. Walls made of SIPs result in a house that's nearly twice as thermally resistant and draft free as conventional wood-frame construction.

The structure was initially built virtually, modeled in 3D to verify assembly and connection details. The premanufactured timber frame and SIP wall and roof components resulted in a relatively quick assembly of the building envelope, in less than one month. It took an additional year to complete construction with electrical and plumbing hookups, roofing, siding, and interior work.

The east-facing side of the house is a wall of glass, topped by the butterfly roof that forms a V with the north and south sides. Landscaping is all natural, drought-tolerant native plantings.

TOP LEFT AND RIGHT: A covered rear porch (left) is the perfect place to enjoy the area's natural beauty. Radiant floor heating coils were cast into the slab in the screened porch (right) so that the space could be converted to interior living space in the future.

BOTTOM: An open floor plan accommodates cooking, dining, and living areas in a single public space. The roof is pitched high, and its glass wall opens to beautiful views of forest surrounding the house.

ABOVE: A sculptured black solid-stone bathtub and shower dominate one end of the master bathroom. Carved from a solid piece of granite, the tub fills from water cascading from a spout in the ceiling. Shower water drains through the river rock pebble mat in the floor. A separate rainwater showerhead provides a memorable showering experience.

ABOVE: The white subway-tile backsplash and white cabinets contrast with the dark brown kitchen walls. Countertops are sturdy, long-lasting butcher block, while the floor is polished concrete with exposed aggregate to create a high-sheen reflective surface.

HEATING AND COOLING

The house has an electric boiler to provide heat for the radiant floor heating system. Electric heating is an environmentally friendly choice in this area because of the significant wind energy that powers the electric grid located in eastern Washington. With natural ventilation and breezes off Puget Sound, the house requires no air-conditioning. Large overhangs prevent direct sun from warming the house uncomfortably in summer but allow the sun to help heat the house in the winter when the sun is lower in the sky. Concrete floors serve as thermal mass, absorbing the heat from the sun and gently releasing it over time.

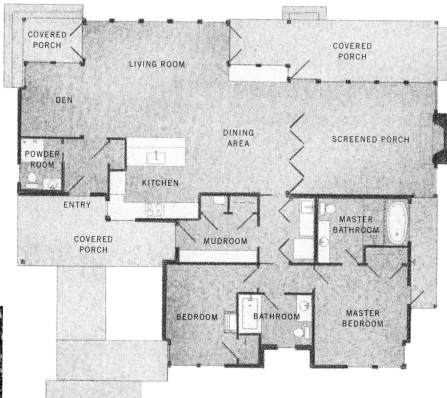

The house under construction, with the timber frame erected. The next step will be to attach the SIPs.

Photo courtesy of FabCab

GREEN FEATURES
- Flexible spaces
- Recycled metal roof
- Concrete floors
- No carpeting
- Dual-flush toilets
- Locally sourced materials as available
- Materials with recycled content
- Composting bin
- Drought-tolerant native plantings

ENERGY-EFFICIENT FEATURES
- Daylighting
- High-efficiency windows
- Large roof overhangs
- Natural cross ventilation
- HRV
- Radiant heat
- Tankless water heater
- Air sealing
- SIPs
- LED and CFL lighting
- ENERGY STAR–rated appliances

THE PROPERTY AS A SANCTUARY

The house and driveway are located on about 1.4 acres. The couple's remaining 7.9 acres are in a Forestry Management Plan, specifically the Public Benefits Rating System (PBRS), with King County; PBRS offers an incentive to preserve open space on private property in the county by providing a tax reduction. Sara and Jed have agreed to maintain it in a natural state.

The land is densely wooded native forest (Douglas fir, madrona, cedar, huckleberry, salmonberry, etc.) that houses countless bird, mammal, and amphibian species. Native animals include eagles, nesting owls, pileated woodpeckers, deer, salamanders, newts, Pacific tree frogs, and snakes. The site is in a continuous state of improvement so that it will become even more favorable for wildlife. Owl nest boxes, birdhouses, and a bat house have been installed, and a wildlife ecosystem pond is in the planning stage.

The property is waterfront and has a trail that meanders a quarter mile through the woods to their beach on Quartermaster Harbor. The house currently serves as the owners' vacation home but it may become their primary residence when they retire.

According to Emory, "The finished home fits well with the newer Pacific Northwest regional style that tends to have sloping roofs, clean lines, and exposed wood. This home is a modern adaptation of timber frame construction. People tend to like it for its blending of contemporary forms with the warmth of wood (and its time-tested way of building)."

A folding wall closes off the screened porch or opens the dining room up to it in mild weather. Douglas fir on the folding doors matches the timbers and the window and door trim.

OPERABLE GLASS WALL SYSTEMS

Glass wall systems made of folding walls offer unobstructed views and daylighting when closed and create a large indoor–outdoor space with fresh air ventilation when open. Some systems have almost invisible tracks in the ceiling or floor. They offer good insulation as well as excellent natural light. The glass wall in the Vashon Island House opens up the screened porch to the rest of the public living areas.

Folding glass walls are available in various configurations, folding to the left, to the right, or bifold applications that split to fold in two directions. The walls can bifold inward or outward, can stack or be frameless, and can be visible or disappear into the wall. These walls can be used in interior or exterior spaces, and many manufacturers offer walls that meet high-velocity hurricane zone (HVHZ) requirements.

Operable glass wall frames are available in a variety of materials, and the glass comes in clear, opaque, frosted, privacy glass, and so on. Some walls are custom made to meet specifications of an individual space; others come in standard sizes. For more information about the wall system used in the Vashon House, visit the NanaWall website (nanawall.com).

LAKE UNION FLOATING HOME

Unique hybrid
construction

PHOTOGRAPHERS
Steve Keating (except
where noted)

ARCHITECT
E. Cobb Architects

BUILDER
Little and Little
Construction

STRUCTURAL
ENGINEERS
Harriott Valentine
Engineers
Swenson Say Faget

LOCATION
Lake Union, Wash.

SIZE
1,842 sq. ft.

FACING PAGE: Wind, rain,
and spray are no match
for the exterior cladding
of fiber cement panels.
The screen in the corner
of the house is made of
hardy tropical ipé (see
p. 155) and forms an
enclosure for bicycle
storage. The common
dock in the foreground
is used to get from the
floating home back to
dry land.

BUILDING A FLOATING HOME IS A UNIQUE WAY FOR a couple to downsize after sending two children off to college. This couple wanted to live smaller and spend time on or near water. They decided to build this house as their main residence on Lake Union in Seattle.

The house took a year to build, begun in January 2013 and completed in January 2014. The entire house—from the flotation base to finishes and accessories—was built in the Port Townsend Boatyard. Once complete it was towed and moored to its permanent location on Lake Union where it was ready for occupation right after it was connected to sewer, electricity, and gas and was given all the necessary inspections and permits.

KEEPING THE HOUSE AFLOAT

In the design stage it was important to make sure the house would be buoyant. A meticulous weight tally had to be done, weighing everything from structure, glass, finishes, and appliances to plumbing fixtures, furnishings, and personal items—all that the boat would have to keep afloat.

Everything the design team could assign a weight value to was accounted for. By adding up all the parts of the house structure, designers determined a total of 58.8 tons (the mostly below-water flotation structure was weighed separately). Based on that tonnage, the float engineer then used a weight distribution diagram to design the hollow concrete float that would provide stability and a level platform with a 1 ft. 8 in. freeboard—the distance between a ship's waterline and deck (or in this case, the distance between its waterline and first floor). Once the house was permanently moored and furnished, divers strategically placed polyethylene drums beneath the float to carefully fine-tune its leveling.

BUILDING ON DRY LAND

Having access to a marine travel lift enabled dry land construction (see the top photo on p. 154), which was much more efficient and precise than building directly on a flotation structure. Because of the unique demands of a floating house, a combination of residential construction tradesmen and ship builders worked together to build it.

A local aluminum boatbuilder executed the exterior metalwork. While aluminum was his preferred working material, he also was persuaded to fabricate the interior steel stair, rails, fireplace surround, and float hatch. Several of the carpenters had extensive wood boat construction experience. Whether boatbuilders or carpenters, all involved in the construction were people who love the sea, which shows in every detail of the house.

A wall of glass fills the living room, dining room, and kitchen with natural light, while in the right corner and behind the sofa, operable glass panels allow air to circulate, cooling hot days. A large overhang and heat lamp over the outdoor dining table make the deck usable on cool evenings—even during drizzly Seattle winters.

FIBER CEMENT SIDING

Fiber cement siding is an increasingly popular exterior cladding material. Made of sand, cement, and cellulose fibers, it comes primed, stained, painted, or as raw siding in lap siding, panels, and shingles. It is also available smooth or textured with a look of wood, stucco, stone, or brick.

The siding is more durable and less expensive than wood and works particularly well in hot, humid climates where siding is prone to rot and fungus.

Because it doesn't have knots and other inconsistencies of wood, fiber cement siding is more durable and holds paint better, which reduces maintenance costs. In addition to low maintenance, the siding resists moisture, termites, warping, shrinking, cracking, fading, other insect damage, fire, and impact damage. The James Hardie® siding used on this house has a 30-year warranty. For more information, visit the manufacturer's website (jameshardie.com).

Curtains of aluminum chain mail glow with light while keeping the large kitchen space private. The backsplash is marble, and the countertops are quartz.

Given the defined above- and below-volume area limits, the design challenge was to carve out the required exterior spaces without overly compressing interior spaces. Carefully parceling out the volume, engineers created usable exterior spaces and openings above water (such as the top-level deck with Jacuzzi® and fire pit), while balancing the weight of the remaining mass with the buoyancy created by the maximum water displacement of the float.

The tight urban pressures of the dock location required the use of every inch of space, using precise nautical management of weight and materials. It also required a unique home delivery process, using contractors, ship builders, massive shipyard equipment, and a tug.

TAKING THE HOUSE TO SEA

Once fully assembled in the shipyard, a maritime crew took over the delivery of the home to its final destination. According to architect Eric Cobb, "The

ENGINEERED FLOORING

Engineered wood is an environmentally friendly alternative to solid-wood flooring that requires cutting down fewer trees and creates less waste. With a core made of stable wood fiber covered with a choice of wood veneers, the flooring minimizes expansion and shrinkage due to temperature and humidity changes.

Engineered floors are also more versatile than solid wood. They can be installed as floating (which means they're connected to each other but not fastened to the floor), nailed, or glued down. They can go below, on, or above grade (solid wood can't be installed below grade). They can also be installed on floors where only thin flooring will fit. A variety of species of wood is available. Further information about the engineered oak floor in this house is available from Kentwood Floors™ (kentwoodfloors.com/us).

TRIPLE-GLAZED WINDOWS

Window construction has come a long way since the days when only a single pane of glass stood between the inside of a house and the weather outside. Today, improvements include double- and triple-glazed windows (even four-pane windows exist) with low-emissivity coatings (to reduce lost heat), warm-edge spacers to avoid cold bridges (also known as thermal bridges, which are weak spots in insulation), and inert gas (argon or krypton) filling the space between the panes.

The U-value (a measure of heat gain or loss) has improved between single and double-gazed windows from about 1.03 to about 0.43 (the lower the number, the more efficient the window). Triple-glazed windows bring that U-value down to about 0.2 (or lower) and also significantly reduce noise pollution. The only downside to triple-glazed windows is that the view through the glass may be distorted. The most important reason to use triple-glazed windows is the comfort they provide inside the home, in addition to the energy conserved for heating and cooling. For more information about the triple-glazed windows used on this house, visit Fleetwood's website (fleetwood usa.net).

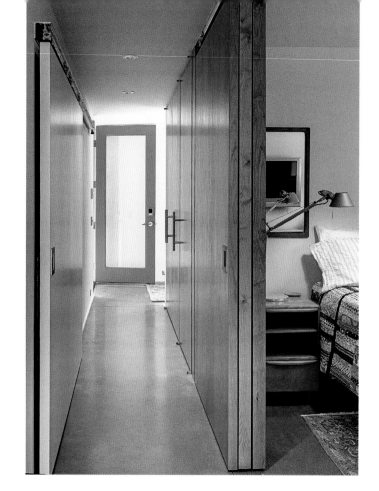

TOP: Sliding doors add flexibility to the interior space. Here the doors open to the multipurpose room, which has been set up as a bedroom, where a guest rising in the morning will set her feet onto a warm concrete floor of radiant heat. The laundry alcove hides behind the sliding door on the left.

BOTTOM: Lovely lake views through a wall of glass make waking up in the first-floor bedroom a beautiful experience. Right outside the bedroom windows a moorage platform of high-strength aluminum grating provides the first step toward the day's adventure.

ABOVE: With its terrific views of the lake and the bridge, the upper deck is a wonderful spot to soak in the hot tub. A built-in fire pit eases the nighttime chill.

ABOVE: Radiant-heat concrete bathroom floors are a warm place to put cold feet in this simple but luxurious bathroom. The vanity cabinet is custom made of alder.

actual immersion of the home into the water was a tense moment." The house and the flotation structure it would be set on were calculated to weigh 168 tons; the actual weight determined by the transit lift was 174 tons. Fortunately, the designers had allowed for slight differences in weight. "When the lift finally released all support in the water, and the structure floated as planned, buoyance never looked so good," Eric said.

In calm seas at low tide, a tug pushed the house for 10 hours through Puget Sound toward Seattle. Traveling early in the morning through the Ballard Locks into Lake Union, the house was delivered to its mooring.

To moor the house, the couple purchased a slip in a 12-home floating community. With a limited number of floating home slips available in Seattle (approximately 500 total), and code stipulations preventing the creation of more, these water dwellings are unique, highly desired, and highly regulated.

SPECIAL FEATURES OF A SPECIAL HOUSE

One of the unique features of the house is the staircase, which provides splendid views from every level. The two-story-high window south of the stair landing exposes a gigantic steel moorage pile and slivers of water and dock. The window at the mid-landing provides a glimpse of the neighbors' dinghy and Lake Union. And from the top landing, there are views of a boat marina and a silhouette of the I-5 bridge.

Because of the small footprint, the house had to be designed to make full use of all the available space. Hallways are minimized and rooms were designed with lots of storage so additional furniture would not be necessary. An open floor plan and carefully placed windows help create the light and open feel the owners desired.

The house has radiant floor heating and no mechanical cooling system. In the heat of summer, multiple large sliding doors on both levels of the north elevation provide and promote air movement off the lake, keeping the house comfortable.

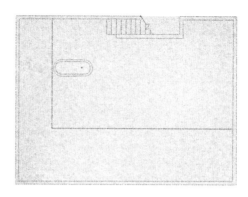

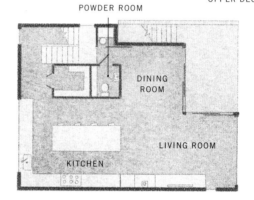
UPPER DECK

POWDER ROOM

DINING ROOM

LIVING ROOM

KITCHEN

SECOND FLOOR

BEDROOM

W/D

BATHROOM

BEDROOM

DECK

BATHROOM

FIRST FLOOR

TOP: The house was built in a Port Townsend boatyard that had access to a marine travel lift.

BOTTOM: The house was then towed most of the 50 miles from the boatyard to its new home in Lake Union. It was pushed for the last 4 miles because the tugboat needed more control and maneuverability in the narrow passages leading up to the lake. The move took about 10 hours.

Photos courtesy of E. Cobb Architects

GREEN FEATURES
- Engineered flooring NAUF
- Quartz countertops
- GREENGUARD-certified kitchen materials
- Low-flow toilets
- Recycled materials

ENERGY-EFFICIENT FEATURES
- Large overhangs
- Triple-pane windows
- Radiant floor heating
- Mini-split system
- LED lighting
- ENERGY STAR–rated appliances

Boats glide right up to the house to anchor at the moorage platform in front of the glass-lined bedroom. A staircase on the second-floor dining deck rises to the rooftop deck, where glass guardrails face the lake and patterned aluminum guardrails give privacy to the middle deck that faces the neighbors.

IPÉ

Ipé (pronounced *e-pay*) is one of three readily available tropical hardwoods from Brazil. (The other two are cumaru and garapa.) A rapidly growing species, ipé reaches maturity at heights of about 120 ft. in approximately 35 years. Ipé is about 2½ times harder than oak and is Class A fire rated. It is naturally resistant to rot, decay, termites, scratches, and splintering without being treated with chemi-

cals. Most ipé is dark brown, but it weathers to a silvery gray unless sealer is applied to retain the natural color. This wood is used for siding, interior flooring, window frames, and decking (it is usually less expensive than composite decking). Much of the ipé available today is with FSC or other sustainable-yield chains of command.

OLDE SEAWATCH

Modular

PHOTOGRAPHER
Michael Rinko,
Jump Visual

DESIGNER
Ryan Scott Meyers,
Atlantic Modular
Builders

BUILDER
Atlantic Modular
Builders

MANUFACTURER
Excel Homes®

LOCATION
Manasquan, N.J.

SIZE
1,800 sq. ft.

FACING PAGE: To make
the most of views of
the Atlantic Ocean just
across the street from
the house, the family
located the main living
area on the top level.
Outside the living room,
a spacious third-floor
porch—where the fam-
ily spends much of its
time—opens wide to take
in the views.

FOR YEARS AND YEARS, AN OLD BEACH BUNGALOW
sat on this narrow lot and served as a place where a family's summer
memories were made. While the owners valued the bungalow as a summer home, they were anxious for an upgrade, with the intention to one
day tear the beach house down and build their dream retirement home
overlooking the ocean. When the couple's two daughters left for college,
the time suddenly seemed right for the now-retired parents to follow
through on their dream. What had been used only for summer vacations
became their primary retirement residence.

Given the proximity to the beach and ocean, the owners wanted to
make the most of the views, so the builder suggested setting the house as
a "reverse living" home, where the bedrooms are on the floor below the
kitchen and great room area. This layout allows the couple to experience
the ocean views from the family room where they enjoy entertaining.
Given that the main living level is three floors up, they installed an elevator.

REPLACING A HOUSE DAMAGED BY SANDY

The initial existing beach bungalow flooded during Hurricane Sandy.
At the time, the couple repaired the house so they could keep using it
while they took some time to plan their new home, which they built two
years later.

The couple hired Atlantic Modular Builders to create their new home,
but it wasn't going to be a standard teardown and rebuild. Atlantic Modular worked with Mazza Demolition & Recycling to recycle the existing
house, which would be demolished. Mazza accepts 200,000 tons of bulk
waste and construction debris a year, about 10 tons for this project. Workers sort through the debris at its facility, separating out the recyclables
such as wood, concrete, and scrap metal, with the remainder of the rubble
becoming biofuel.

BUILDING MODULAR

The couple had watched Atlantic Modular put up other houses in the area
and decided that modular construction would be the best way to go for
their new house. By building modular, they could start and complete the
house without missing a summer season. It took five days to build the
house in the factory and then 20 weeks from set to completion.

The house is 18 ft. wide on a lot that's only 24 ft. wide. The modules are
stacked back to back, as opposed to side by side like most narrow modular buildings. Their house has four modules per floor. The widest a single
modular could be was 15 ft. 9 in., so the only way to take full advantage of

A direct-vent gas fireplace helps warm the house on the coldest days, while in warmer months ceiling fans and sliding doors keep the house cool and comfortable.

the available width of the building was to stack the units back to back.

Ryan Scott Meyers, design manager of Atlantic Modular Builders, says that modular houses typically provide 10% savings compared to a conventionally built house of comparable size and quality. But with tightly built and insulated modulars, the savings continue: "Once the home is complete the owners should see a savings in their energy bills due to the high insulation values of the modular homes we build," Ryan said.

BUILDING IN ENERGY EFFICIENCY

The Olde Seawatch house was designed with lots of energy-efficient windows because the owners wanted to make the most of the natural ocean breezes (obviously, in cold weather those energy-efficient windows come in very handy). ENERGY STAR–rated ceiling fans move the ocean air throughout the house, which limits the need for

mechanical HVAC equipment. At the time of writing, the house hadn't yet been through a yearly cycle, but the builders expect energy bills to be much less than other residences in the area because of the excellent insulation in the walls of the house.

BUILDING TO FEMA REQUIREMENTS

An additional cost to the owners was raising the house above the government-mandated floodplain. However, this also provided a benefit because it allowed the owners to use the area under the house for off-street parking and storage.

The ground level was totally outfitted with water-friendly materials, such as resilient wood stairs made from a hybrid of two species of *Eucalyptus urophylla* trees (sold as Lyptus®), concrete floors, fiber cement sheathing, and mold-resistant drywall. This means that future floodwaters could penetrate the ground level of the house without ruining the structure.

At the rear of the third floor the light-filled kitchen opens to the living room. Countertops are natural granite, and cabinets are constructed of plywood and painted bright white.

PERMEABLE PAVING

Permeable paving allows water to drain into the ground and in the process to filter out pollutants and contaminants, preventing the pooling of rainwater and reducing the amount of pollutants that enters natural waterways from runoff. The initial cost for permeable pavers is generally higher than for traditional paving materials, but they will likely reduce the cost of other drainage and storm water management systems on the property—and add to curb appeal.

Several types of systems are available. Some are as simple as mulches, such as pebbles, gravel, and sod. More sophisticated systems are pavers of concrete, cut stone, or rugged plastic molded with voids where grass can grow or where water can sim-

ply drain through. These materials may be indistinguishable from nonporous resources and come in a wide variety of colors, textures, and styles.

Snow and ice removal present a challenge to using permeable paving in cold climates. For example, sand used on icy streets may clog the openings. In addition, road salt containing chlorides can filter down into the water system, and plowing may destroy the integrity of the pavers. A maintenance program is necessary when using these permeable systems in snowy areas.

For further information about the permeable pavers used in this house, visit the Unilock® website (unilock.com); for additional resources, visit PaverSearch™ (paversearch.com).

In good weather, the third-floor balcony, with its ocean view and sea breezes, is an extension of the indoor living space. The decking on the balcony is fiberglass.

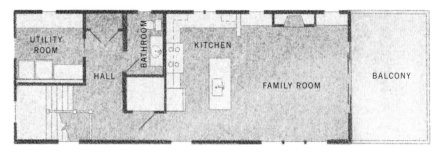

THIRD FLOOR

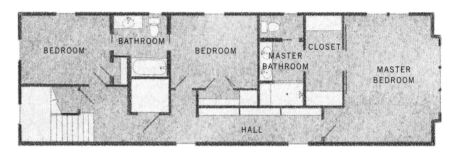

SECOND FLOOR

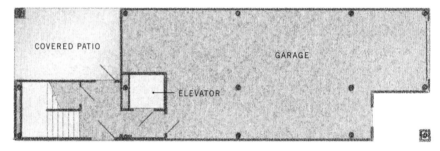

LOWER LEVEL

GREEN FEATURES
- Recycled metal roof
- FSC-certified wood
- WaterSense fixtures (see the facing page)
- Low-flow shower and faucets
- Low water consumption toilets
- Insulation with recycled content
- Recycled materials from demolished beach house
- Unrecycled construction debris turned into biofuel
- Permeable paving

ENERGY-EFFICIENT FEATURES
- Large overhangs
- Gas furnace with 95%+ efficiency
- ENERGY STAR–rated tankless water heater
- LED lighting
- ENERGY STAR–rated appliances
- ENERGY STAR–rated ceiling fans

ABOVE: Rustic barn doors add a country touch to the master bedroom. A clerestory window and a large side window with a window seat flood the room with light and offer plenty of fresh air.

RIGHT: The entrance hall to the second-floor bedroom level functions as a wall of shelves, a storage area for books and a way to display decorative items.

WaterSense label.

WATERSENSE

WaterSense® is both a voluntary water-efficiency program and a label the U.S. Environmental Protection Agency (EPA) allows companies to use on products that have been independently certified to conform to WaterSense specifications for efficiency and performance. A showerhead or toilet that bears the WaterSense label is proof for consumers that the product was tested and met EPA criteria of water efficiency and performance.

The idea behind the program is to encourage water conservation. This is a voluntary program, but everyone building a new house, remodeling an existing one, or simply replacing a bathroom faucet wants to save water, while both saving money and making an ecofriendly choice.

Products that qualify for the WaterSense label include bathroom sink faucets, showerheads, toilets, and flushing urinals. For additional information, see the U.S. Department of Energy's website (epa.gov/WaterSense).

HILLTOP HOUSE

Timber Frame/Panelized

PHOTOGRAPHER
Great Island
Photography

ARCHITECT
Randall Walter

BUILDER/
MANUFACTURER
Bensonwood

LANDSCAPE ARCHITECT
Daniel W. Bruzga

BLOWER DOOR TEST
1.0 ACH50

LOCATION
Hillsborough, N.H.

SIZE
2,000 sq. ft.

FORREST AND JULIA ALWAYS KNEW THEY WANTED to build a small house sometime in their future. And they knew where they wanted to build it—on property they purchased overlooking a beautiful lake. For 10 years they spent their summers in a camper on the site, moving it here and there to decide which part of the lot would make the best location for their future home. This gave them time to decide exactly where they wanted the house, what views they wanted, and what features should be included in the design.

Forrest and Julia wanted a high-performance house that could be built quickly. Once they were ready, they chose builder Bensonwood. Ultimately, the company met their expectations, coming through with a very efficient house built in only five months that became the couple's primary residence.

CONSTRUCTING THE HOUSE

The homeowners chose Bensonwood not only because of its excellent reputation but also because of its Open-Built® system, which "disentangles the systems of the timber frame house," according to Forrest. As with any house, things eventually break and need fixing. So the couple reasoned that if the house needed to be modified in the future, it would be less complicated and costly if they had easy access to the mechanical systems. "Most timber frame houses are particularly clunky at getting to any of the mechanicals after construction is completed," Forrest quipped.

The Open-Built concept means that mechanicals are separated from the structure for easy access. This adaptability allows the house to evolve along with the changing needs of occupants and to accommodate new and improved technologies. Renovations are done efficiently with minimal disruption and waste, helping ensure that the home remains useful and relevant long into the future.

Bensonwood refers to their construction technique as "montage building," meaning that the house is built virtually first, then fabricated into a relatively few panelized assemblies that can be shipped flat and rapidly assembled on site with minimal disruption to the land.

HEATING AND COOLING

The high-performance envelope enclosing the house means it takes far less energy to heat than a standard house. The masonry heater (see p. 165) in the center of the main floor is loaded with firewood once a day and keeps the house warm for 24 hours, even in New Hampshire's coldest months. Solar panels heat the 80-gal. water tank, which provides hot

The north-facing front of the house has the fewest windows so the house won't lose heat in the cold New Hampshire winters. The gravel path allows rainwater to seep into the earth and prevents pooling.

ABOVE: The larger opening in the masonry heater is the firebox and the upper door is a baking oven that the owners use to make pizza. The countertops are soapstone, the flooring is birch, and the cabinets are cherry.

RIGHT: The masonry heater is in the middle of the open floor plan and can warm the whole first floor and the master suite above via a radiant floor panel on the second floor.

ABOVE: A rolling barn door between the master bedroom and bathroom adds a rustic touch and frees space that a swinging door would take up. Skylights add light and warmth to the room.

LEFT: The master bath includes a separate area for a soaking tub, which gets a lot of use during the long New Hampshire winter. The tub surround and vanity top are soapstone, echoing the counter-top material in the kitchen.

MASONRY HEATERS

Masonry heaters are a highly efficient method of heating and have warmed people for thousands of years. Fire within the masonry structure heats the dense thermal mass of brick, stone, or concrete, which stores and slowly radiates its heat outward, warming a room for hours even after the fire burns out.

Because masonry heaters burn at such a high temperature, they emit less pollution. For this house, the masonry heater is the primary source of heat during the cold New Hampshire winter. It heats the main living space and the master bedroom above, maintaining the house at a comfortable 68° to 70°F throughout the winter.

Homeowner Forrest typically fires the heater once a day, and the 900° heat from the burn slowly pushes out through the brick and soapstone to provide 24 hours of radiant heat. Incredibly efficient and clean, the burner heats the house on a little more than three cords of wood a year. For further information, visit the Masonry Heater Association's website (mha-net.org)

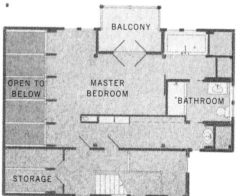

SECOND FLOOR

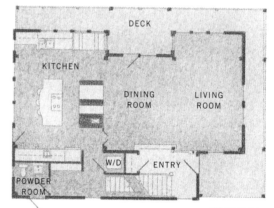

FIRST FLOOR

STACK-EFFECT COOLING

Stack-effect cooling, also known as the chimney effect, is passive natural ventilation that occurs when warmer, less-dense indoor air rises out the top of a structure and draws in denser, cooler air from below. This effect occurs because of the temperature difference and creates a natural flow. Towers or chimneys can carry air up and out, and extra height enhances the effect. Skylights or clerestory windows can also serve the same purpose.

To create the stack effect in a house, air requires an open route from the lower inlet to the outlet at the top of the structure. Both inlet and outlet ports should be adjustable to control cooling. In some cases this function is controlled by thermostats to optimize system performance. Stack-effect cooling is inexpensive to install, uses no energy, and is low maintenance.

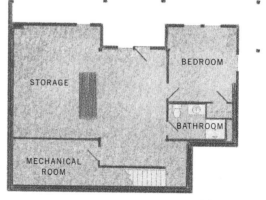

LOWER LEVEL

water from mid-March through early October. A wall-mounted propane furnace makes hot water during the winter months as well as radiant heat for the walk-out basement and backup radiant heat for the remainder of the house.

Except for a window unit in the master bedroom, which is only occasionally needed, the house is not air-conditioned. The owners open the bedroom sky-lights and the awning windows, which open into the cathedral space above the island in the kitchen. Opening the double-hung windows on the south kitchen wall creates a natural cooling chimney or stack effect (see the facing page) in the evening. Because so much of the house is glass, triple cellular window shades control heat loss and gain.

CAPTURING BEAUTIFUL LAKE VIEWS

To make the most of the lake views the couple chose a broad-faced Cape-style house form. This gave them the most expansive view from the living room, dining room, and kitchen. Because the ridge runs perpendicular to the lake, runoff from rain and snow sheds on the sides of the house away from the best views.

Forrest finds it difficult to sum up in mere words what their home means to them. "Perhaps it can be measured in our reluctance to leave it during vaca-tion, or the way it always welcomes us back each evening when we return from our working sojourn. It plays such an important part in our lives that Julia left her job in order to be able to work from home."

"We love it year round. Every day seems like a vacation during the summertime, and in the cold dark winter it shelters us from the elements by wrapping us in warmth and light."

SOAPSTONE COUNTERTOPS

Soapstone is a durable, dense, nonporous, maintenance-free material that's resistant to bac-teria, stains, acids, chemicals, wine, and hot pots. Available in a variety of textures and dimensions, soapstone has a natural blue-gray color, which acquires a darker sheen with regular oiling.

Architectural-grade soapstone used for counter-tops has a lower talc content and is harder than artist-grade soapstone used for carving. The cost is comparable to other natural stone, such as granite, but the slabs are generally smaller (7 ft. or less) so seams may be necessary on very large counters. Soapstone can get scratched and nicked, but these can be removed by buffing with fine sandpaper. The soapstone in this house is from Vermont Soapstone (vermontsoapstone.com).

JOHNS ISLAND HOME

SIPs

PHOTOGRAPHER
Margaret Rambo

ARCHITECT
Sam Rashkin

BUILDER
Amerisips® Contractors

MANUFACTURER
Extreme Panel

INTERIOR DESIGNER
Amerisips Design Group

BLOWER DOOR TEST
2.3 ACH50

HERS INDEX
1

CERTIFICATIONS
ENERGY STAR Version 3
EPA Indoor airPLUS
Leadership in Energy
and Environmental
Design™ (LEED®)
Platinum
U.S. Department of
Energy Zero Energy
Ready Home

LOCATION
Johns Island, S.C.

SIZE
2,085 sq. ft.

AFTER CONSTRUCTING SITE-BUILT HOMES FOR several years, Amerisips owners Steve and Tina Bostic began researching better ways to build. They discovered SIPs and started experimenting with greener, high-performance construction methods. To control the building quality, the Bostics decided to provide in-house architecture, mechanical engineering, interior design, and construction services.

When empty nesters Barbara and Robert decided to downsize and build a new home for themselves they asked the Bostics for help. The couple wanted a home that would meet their new lifestyle needs, with large public areas for entertaining and smaller sleeping areas.

BUILDING WITH SIPS

Barbara and Robert chose to build their new home with SIPs because they wanted to reduce their carbon footprint, limit their energy use, and reduce utility costs. Their former, much larger house had been modular built, so they were already familiar and comfortable with prefab construction.

Steve recommended they build a house that met both the DOE Zero Energy Ready Home program (see p. 172) and the U.S. Green Building Council® LEED Platinum® level. Barbara and Robert knew there would be a small cost increase to build such an efficient house. But they were okay with that possibility because they would earn both federal and state tax credits, as well as save $200 to $300 per month on energy costs.

DURABILITY AND ENERGY SAVING

Because of the high hurricane potential in South Carolina, the house was built to endure winds of 160 mph or more, using sturdy SIPs and double-pane, impact-resistant window glass coated to minimize heat transfer. In 1989 Hurricane Hugo had devastating effects on this area, and in recent years one of Amerisips new houses took a direct hit from a tornado—happily with no resulting structural damage.

To reach the difficult-to-attain HERS 1 rating, the Bostics had to take every measure possible to build a house that would minimize energy use. So the house is equipped with PV panels to provide energy and solar hot water panels for domestic hot water. About 90% of the lighting is ENERGY STAR rated and/or uses LED lights. The refrigerator, dishwasher, washing machine, and ceiling fans are all ENERGY STAR rated. The air-to-water heat pump provides both heated and cooled air and supplements the domestic hot water supply. The air is distributed throughout the house via a small-duct high-velocity (SDHV) system (see p. 173), which has con-

The siding of this cottage-style house is fiber cement clapboard and shingles, materials that are durable and require minimal maintenance. The roofing is asphalt shingles.

High ceilings give the house a bigger feel than its 2,000 sq. ft. The floors throughout the house are bamboo, except for the bathrooms, which are tile.

siderably less leakage than a traditional vented system. The SDHV system is not only very efficient but also quieter than a typical forced-air system and creates an even, draft-free interior environment.

AN AWARD-WINNING HOUSE

In addition to all of the home's certifications, the house has also won awards for its efficiency. It received a U.S. Department of Energy (DOE) Housing Innovation Award in the Custom Builder Award category and the Best Contractor/Builder—Small Award as part of the U.S. Green Building Council's national Best of Building Awards.

RIGHT: The fireplace on the back wall of the living room is a gas Heatilator®, which supplements the heating system on chilly days.

BELOW: Kitchen countertops are hard-wearing granite, and appliances are ENERGY STAR rated. The clear-glass light fixture above the island adds visual interest while maintaining the open feel of the space.

ZERO ENERGY READY HOME PROGRAM

The DOE Zero Energy Ready Home program (formerly called the DOE Challenge Home) was established in 2008 to acknowledge houses that meet demanding requirements for energy savings, comfort, health, and durability. The program requires that designated houses meet the ENERGY STAR for Homes Version 3 standards, along with proven Building America innovations. The house must be 40% to 50% more energy efficient than a typical home, which corresponds to a HERS Index in the 50s (see "Home Energy Rating System" on p. 193), according to an approved third party. Very specific requirements govern windows, insulation, hot water systems, duct systems, and indoor air quality. A full list of program requirements is available from the Department of Energy's website (energy.gov/eere/buildings/zero-energy-ready-home).

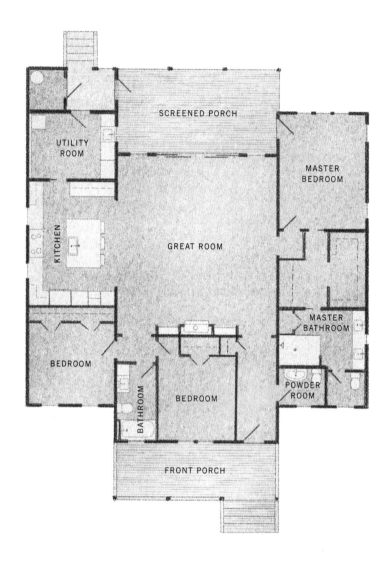

GREEN FEATURES
- Bamboo flooring
- Dual-flush toilets
- Viega® PureFlow® water system
- Low-flow faucets and showers
- Low- or no-VOC paints and finishes

ENERGY-EFFICIENT FEATURES
- PV panels
- Solar hot water panels
- Large overhangs
- SDHV system
- ERV
- High-efficiency air-to-water heat pump
- LED and CFL lighting
- ENERGY STAR–rated appliances
- ENERGY STAR–rated ceiling fans

The idea of having not too much but just enough space kept the master bedroom to a relatively small dimension, according to the owners' needs.

The rear screened porch doesn't need to be winterized for year-round use because the climate is so mild. And when the weather gets very hot, ENERGY STAR–rated ceiling fans help keep the homeowners cool.

SMALL-DUCT HIGH-VELOCITY (SDHV) SYSTEMS

ENERGY STAR (energystar.gov) estimates that 20% to 30% of the air that moves through residential ductwork is lost through "leaks, holes, and poorly connected ducts," accounting for a major loss of energy.

Small- or mini-duct systems are a different story. Because the ducts in these systems are significantly smaller than traditional systems, there is less surface area for energy loss. Unlike most sheet-metal ducts, mini-ducts are insulated, and their joints are much tighter, often connected with gaskets. Depending on the manufacturer, HV ducts leak no more than 5% of the air forced through them, if they leak at all.

SDHV systems use smaller and less noticeable outlets, often several per room, so that air is evenly distributed. These flexible, insulated feeder ducts are only 2 in. to 3 in. in diameter, and air moves through them at about 1,500 ft. per minute (fpm) compared with 500 fpm to 600 fpm in standard ductwork. High pressure also eliminates dust buildup within the ducts, which improves indoor air quality.

This more efficient system includes an air handler that works with a home's boiler, central air-conditioning system, geothermal system, or heat pump to reduce humidity by about a third when cooling, compared to conventional duct systems, requiring less energy. SDHV systems also lower relative humidity when in the heating mode, reducing the need for higher thermostat settings.

Mini-ducts eliminate unsightly registers and radiators and more evenly circulate air. The systems are installed in new homes and can easily be retrofitted into older homes during renovation. The National Trust for Historic Preservation® endorses Unico System®, the company that supplied the system for the Johns Island Home. Initial installation costs can be high, but homeowners save over the life of the system and their indoor environments are more comfortable. For further information about the system used in this house, visit Unico's website (unicosystemgreen.com) or HighVelocityHelper.com™.

HALCYON
HILL

Component

PHOTOGRAPHER
Patrick Barta
Photography

ARCHITECT/
MANUFACTURER
Lindal® Cedar Homes

GENERAL CONTRACTOR
Owner

LOCATION
British Columbia,
Canada

SIZE
2,100 sq. ft.

FACING PAGE: The house
has five asphalt roof-
lines, each of which is
pitched toward a center
drain that leads water
to a lower roof and into
the ground. A planned
rainwater collection sys-
tem will store the water
for irrigation use. The
grounds are landscaped
with boulders and stones
found on the property.

LINDAL CEDAR HOMES IS A UNIQUE COMPANY. IT cuts all of the components for its houses, which can be erected nearly anywhere in the world. Most of the parts are precut in their factory in Burlington, Wash., and doors and windows are prehung. Precisely precut wood components create less waste and require a smaller-than-normal shipping container. Components are numbered, and parts are sent to a local contractor who assembles the home.

To customize a Lindal home, buyers find a plan they like in one of the Lindal planbooks and, working with an architect or their local Lindal dealer, modify it to fit their likes and needs. Customers may also start from scratch with their architect or local Lindal dealer.

To make the kits as versatile as possible, Lindal uses architectural-grade glulam posts and beams throughout a home. With this method of construction, the posts and beams support the roof of the home, which allows most interior walls to be easily moved or removed. The posts and beams rather than the walls bear the structural load.

Jeanne, the owner of the Halcyon Hill house, is a Lindal dealer, so she had a clear idea of both the product and the outcome when she decided to build her own house with Lindal. She was also captivated by the company's environmental priorities. Their recycling program reclaims and recycles much of their construction waste. Jeanne also liked the fact that when the company builds a house, they plant trees to offset the trees that were cut down to mill the lumber that went into the house. Lindal has planted more than 100,000 trees in the names of their customers and in partnership with the American Forests® Global ReLeaf® program (www.americanforests.org).

BUILDING FROM A COMPANY DESIGN

Jeanne admires Lindal's contemporary designs, but she also likes mixing modern with natural elements. As an example, she points to the dining table made of local maple right near the very contemporary black-and-white kitchen counters. She chose one of Lindal's predesigned plans and made some modest modifications. The floor-to-ceiling windows are typical of the company, but Jeanne expanded the loft area to make a cozy area underneath for the family room.

The house took about three months to dry in, or make weathertight. Interior finishes and landscaping took several more months to complete. Jeanne continues to work on the landscaping.

ABOVE: The kitchen cabinets are made from a veneered medium-density fiberboard (MDF). The countertops are quartz, and the appliances are ENERGY STAR rated. The glulam beams in the ceiling extend through the wall to the exterior of the house.

LEFT: The house has views of the Salish Sea, off the southeastern coast of Vancouver Island, between the Strait of Juan de Fuca and the Haro Strait. The North Shore Mountains are beyond. Flooring throughout most of the house, with the exception of the bathrooms, is engineered wood.

FACING PAGE: The soaring ceiling above the living room and dining area gives the house a more expansive feel than its square footage would suggest. The owner obtained the local maple tabletop from a nearby furniture maker; Lindal made the table legs.

HEATING AND COOLING

The envelope of the house was built to high standards of efficiency. Advanced framing was used for the construction along with extra insulation and energy-efficient double-pane windows. The house requires no air-conditioning system because design, material, and construction measures were taken to keep the interior climate naturally comfortable.

Windows in the house provide cross ventilation throughout, with fewer windows on the shadier, colder north side and more abundant windows on the south side. The large overhangs block the high sun during warmer months while allowing the lower winter sun to enter during colder months. Jeanne planted deciduous Japanese maples on the southwest side of the house to block the sun in the summer; they lose their leaves in the winter, allowing in sunlight.

FLEXIBLE SPACE

Doing double-duty, the lower bedroom serves as Jeanne's office but houses a Murphy bed for occasional visitors. The living room has a sleeper couch to provide for additional guests. In her spare time, Jeanne enjoys the serenity of the area, while watching the moon rise over the mountains.

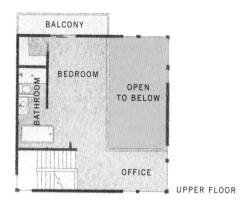

GREEN FEATURES
- Engineered wood floors
- No carpeting
- Quartz countertops
- Low-flow faucets, showerheads, and toilets
- Low-VOC paint and stain
- Recycled plastic grid for permeable paving
- Locally sourced materials

ENERGY-EFFICIENT FEATURES
- Optimal solar orientation
- Large overhangs
- Cross ventilation
- Radiant floor heating
- Tankless hot water
- ICF foundation (see the facing page)
- Advanced framing
- LED lights
- ENERGY STAR–rated appliances
- Ceiling fans
- Solar ready

For now, the upper sleeping area and bathroom serve as the master bedroom. When the owner gets older and stairs become an issue, she may switch to the bedroom on the main level.

INSULATED CONCRETE FORM FOUNDATIONS

For decades, concrete walls and foundations were made the same way. Plywood or just plain boards are built into forms that contain steel reinforcing bars (rebar) and into which wet concrete is poured. When the concrete hardens, or cures, the forms are ripped off to reveal the bare concrete wall or foundation. We've all seen the fossil-like look of wood grain in old concrete.

Today, wood forms are giving way to polystyrene insulated concrete forms, which fit together like giant Lego pieces, stacking to create a very efficient foundation, or envelope, for an entire house. When concrete cures inside the ICFs, the forms stay in place to provide insulation inside and out. Walls generally are between 4 in. and 12 in. thick. Logix® forms, or panels, were used on this house to create the foundation. These interlock, side to side and top to bottom, leaving no gaps. As the panels go up, vertical rebar is installed at close, regular intervals and secured in place. Finally, concrete is slowly poured down through the structure and all voids carefully filled.

"The Logix wall assembly delivers up to 60% lower air infiltration than a traditionally built wall," according to the company. The steel-reinforced concrete core protects the home against fire, hurricanes, and earthquakes. It also reduces noise infiltration. For more information, visit the Logix website (logixicf.com).

BONSALL HOUSE

Modular/Steel Frame

PHOTOGRAPHERS
Daniel Hennessey
(except where noted)

**ARCHITECT/
MANUFACTURER**
Jared Levy and Gordon
Stott Connect Homes

BUILDER
Card Construction
(predelivery on-site
work)

LOCATION:
Bonsall, Calif.

SIZE
2,180 sq. ft.

BEFORE THEY BUILT THEIR VACATION HOUSE IN SAN Diego County, the Freemans would visit the small farm they owned, where they grew avocados, lemons, and sweet limes to sell to local markets. They stayed in an Airstream® trailer on the property but in time decided to build a more permanent home.

OPTING TO BUILD MODULAR
Darrin Freeman had had some experience in building homes conventionally—with all the decisions, headaches, schedule delays, change orders, and so on that go with that process. His experience was that it usually costs twice as much and takes twice as long as initially promised. Given that the Freemans were planning a vacation home, he also saw the additional challenges of having to coordinate the construction of a second home a distance from his primary residence. He imagined a future of weekly trips to Bonsall for possibly close to two years, coordinating all the items he would need to build a home on site.

Building prefab with Connect Homes presented a more streamlined, simpler way to construct his new house, one in which he made all the decisions before production began. Darrin chose Connect Homes because he trusted they could deliver the level of detail and finish that he wanted.

MODULAR ALMOST COMPLETE UNITS
The completion level of modular units varies depending on the factory that builds them and the owner's requirements. The modules built by Connect Homes click together into virtually complete structures, almost like large Lego pieces.

Jared Levy and Gordon Stott of Connect Homes believe it is important to finish as much of the house as possible in the factory, where costs are better controlled and the manufacturer is not at the mercy of weather or local subcontractors' schedules. The Bonsall House took about two months to build in the factory, about three hours to set on site, and then a couple of months to complete on site; it would have been quicker but for a snafu with the original manufacturer.

A SNAFU IN PRODUCTION
Generally, Connect Homes's modular houses are delivered on site almost complete, and within days are nearly ready for move in. Unfortunately for the Freemans, the original manufacturer decided to close their business just when the modules were due to be built. Meanwhile, Darrin and his local general contractor were diligently working on the house's site work.

The siding on this modular vacation house is recycled steel and sustainably harvested western cedar. Large sliding doors on the rear of the house open onto a covered deck, which was also built in the factory. The saltwater pool a few steps away has an integrated spa, which flows into the pool to heat it.

ABOVE: In the stark white kitchen, countertops are quartz with a back-splash of white ceramic subway tiles. The long kitchen island is a favorite gathering spot and a place to sit and admire views of the pool and coastline beyond.

RIGHT: In the corner dining area, the ceiling is a dovetail steel structural panel with a factory-painted white finish. The owner-built boccie court is visible through the sliders.

FACING PAGE: The module above the living room was built without a floor to create the living room's double-height space. The flooring throughout is white oak from sustainably managed forests. Sliding doors on both sides of the living room open to the decks beyond in a seamless flow.

Connect Homes quickly had to find another manufacturer to build the modules. This presented a problem, because few manufacturers are accustomed either to building with steel frames or to building modern homes. The one that agreed to build the "mods" could do only about half of the work. The Connect Home builders would complete the rest on site.

The company was then at the mercy of the scheduling whims of local subcontractors and the weather, the same issues site builders confront

QUARTZ COUNTERTOPS

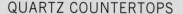

Quartz is one of the hardest and most abundant minerals on earth. It is durable and resists stains, scratches, impact, and heat. It is also nonporous, which means it's resistant to mold and bacteria. As a commonly discarded product of other mining industries, quartz put to good use helps eliminate waste. In short, quartz is a very ecofriendly material, which explains its popularity with environment-conscious homeowners and builders.

The countertop in the Bonsall House is made by Ceasarstone®. To make their countertops, Caesarstone collects waste quartz, which they process, crush, wash, and sift. The panels are then manufactured using quartz aggregate, pigments, and polymers. Like most manufacturers of quartz countertops, Caesarstone offers an abundance of color options. The Caesarstone used in the Bonsall House is certified by GREENGUARD for indoor air quality (see "GREENGUARD Certification Program" p. 115). The company also offers a lifetime warranty on its products. For further information, visit Caesarstone's website (caesarstoneus.com).

TOP: The patio around the pool is poured concrete, and the decking is bamboo. The strategically placed hammock is a great spot to unwind and take in the views.

BOTTOM: A roof sunshade wraps around three sides of the house, including the south and west exposures, to cut down on solar heat gain through windows. A deck pathway leads from the covered front deck to the carport.

With the triple sliding door panels open, the kitchen island feels more like part of the outside. Anybody standing at the island's kitchen sink gets great views of the pool and distant ocean.

TOP: The modules under construction in the factory.

BOTTOM: The modules are lifted with a crane and set on the prepared foundation.

Photos courtesy of Connect Homes

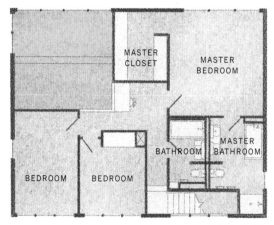

SECOND FLOOR

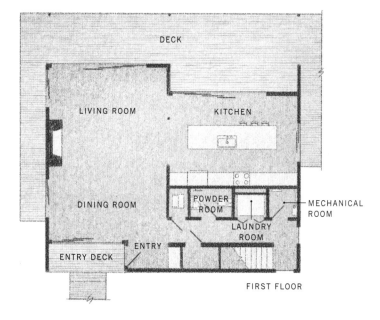

FIRST FLOOR

GREEN FEATURES

- Recycled steel frame and siding
- Recycled bamboo exterior decking
- FSC-certified white oak flooring, NAUF
- Recycled quartz countertops
- Dual-flush/low-flow toilets
- Low-flow faucets and showers
- Low- or no-VOC finishes, paints, adhesives, and primers
- Recycled insulation

ENERGY-EFFICIENT FEATURES

- Cool roof system
- PV system
- High-efficiency glass doors
- Tankless water heater
- Glass wool insulation
- LED and CFL lighting
- High-efficiency washing machine and dishwasher
- ENERGY STAR–rated appliances

On one side of the house is a boccie court and on the other a built in outdoor kitchen.

Photo courtesy of Bryan Chan

when building a conventional home. "Luckily, we had a client who understood the complexities of the process and remained confident that we would still deliver a beautiful, modern home," Jared said.

Since the Bonsall House was built, Connect Homes has opened its own factory to better control the construction process. They will complete 90% to 95% of the building in the factory and shorten the installation time.

LIMITING ENERGY USE

A conventional heat pump forced-air system provides heating and cooling for the house. A PV solar system on the roof keeps the electricity bill as low as $5 a month, even with the pool pumps running. Strategic roof overhangs block the sun in the warmer months but allow light to permeate the house in the winter. Double-glazed windows with a tinted solar film dramatically cut down on heat gain.

The Freemans did all of the landscaping themselves, including building large planter boxes and a full boccie court, over the span of four days. Darrin has since built an extensive outdoor kitchen and outdoor shower. Inside the house, glass is everywhere, and the double-height space makes the house feel light and open—perfectly appropriate for the bluff on which it sits.

A THERMOSTAT THAT LEARNS

The Nest thermostat used in the Bonsall House is a "learning" thermostat. Most computerized thermostats on the market require programming, but the Nest senses a homeowner's preferences and is simple to use. After homeowners have adjusted the thermostat to their liking for about two weeks, Nest takes it from there (although it can still be adjusted by hand, by mobile app, or by computer program). According to Nest, the learning thermostat can be self-installed in about 30 minutes, or homeowners can hire a certified pro installer. Using a smart thermostat saves energy, reduces heating and cooling costs, and keeps the house feeling comfortable without homeowner input. For further information, visit the Nest website (nest.com/thermostat/life-with-nest-thermostat).

WESTPORT BEACH HOUSE

Panelized

PHOTOGRAPHERS
Michael Biondo
Photography (except
where noted)

ARCHITECT
Sellers Lathrop
Architects

BUILDER
The Pratley Company

MANUFACTURER
Bensonwood

BLOWER DOOR TEST
1.21 ACH50

HERS INDEX
47 (see "Home Energy
Rating System" on
p. 193)

CERTIFICATIONS
ENERGY STAR Version 3

LOCATION
Westport, Conn.

SIZE
2,300 sq. ft.

FACING PAGE: The house
fits into the aesthetic of
a quintessential New
England beachfront.
Window shutters were
recycled from the
owner's prior home. The
lower standing-seam
roof reflects the light,
helping keep the porch
cool in the summer.

WHEN MARY JANE LIU REALIZED THAT DAMAGE from 2012's Hurricane Sandy required a teardown of what was left of her old house and construction of a new one, she called architect Ann Lathrop for help.

Mary Jane had already considered prefab construction and was delighted when Ann suggested rebuilding using prefabricated panels. Ann also recommended a great company to work with—Bensonwood. Mary Jane and her daughter drove to New Hampshire to visit the company and were so impressed with the process that they soon hired Bensonwood to build her house.

BUILDING ON A CHALLENGING LOT

Because the lot is small and narrow, Mary Jane wasn't able to use one of Bensonwood's standard designs. Also, stringent height restrictions required her to apply for a variance before building. When the customized design work was done, the shell of the house was built in New Hampshire, shipped to Westport, and raised on the property in about four days. Pratley Company, a local contractor, installed built-ins and ENERGY STAR systems, such as the heating, appliances, and ceiling fans.

BUILDING IN ENERGY EFFICIENCY

Ann was influential in the decision to create an energy-efficient house and coached Mary Jane through what needed to be done to achieve this—even down to the choice of light bulbs. The highly efficient exterior walls contain several inches more insulation than the typical house. Energy-efficient windows installed in those walls also make a significant difference. Thanks to this attention to materials and construction, Mary Jane's gas and electric bills are considerably lower than those of other houses in the area. "The HVAC system works so efficiently that I never have to adjust the thermostat once I program it for the season," she reports.

BUILDING PREFAB

According to Ann, building prefab elements seems logical because quality control and thermal efficiency are typically built into the components. "Site building (or stick building) has been around for hundreds of years, and we are amazed to find contractors doing things the same way, and for the most part this means in an archaic, wasteful, inefficient way of building." It frustrates Ann that there is so much waste on a job site, and she confesses to occasionally going Dumpster® diving to retrieve reusable materials.

ABOVE: The superefficient natural gas direct-vent fireplace in the living area draws its combustion air from outside and does not consume heated air from inside the house, as most traditional fireplaces do. The shelving on either side of the fireplace takes up what otherwise would be wasted space, while also adding another New England feature to the house.

RIGHT: The wall of windows on the southwest side of the house brings plentiful natural light into the kitchen/dining area.

The open layout is conducive to conversation between the cook in the kitchen and her guests in the dining/living area.

SMALL BUT ROOMY

Although Mary Jane needed to keep the house small because of the lot size, she still wanted to pack a lot into its modest footprint, including four bedrooms and three and a half baths. The heavily insulated panelized walls were so thick they robbed some of the interior space, which made the design even more of a challenge, but Ann managed to get it to work.

The first floor would have an open floor plan, the second floor would contain three bedrooms, and a third floor would become the perfect space for her teenage daughter and friends. Down the road, the top floor could become a bunk room for grandchildren. "It was all about creating a house that would be cozy for me alone and at the same time be able to accommodate family and friends who want to visit the beach," she said.

Mary Jane loves everything about her new house: "I know my experience with building a custom paneled house is unique, but I hope that others will learn more about it and commit to such a project to build what I consider a very solid house that is not only very efficient but also storm safe."

ENERGY STAR UPDATED

The ENERGY STAR program was launched in 1992 to improve energy efficiency in everything that uses or conserves energy in the built environment. It's so successful that it has been adopted by Australia, Canada, Japan, New Zealand, Taiwan, and the European Union. And it's no wonder: The EPA says that, through 2014, ENERGY STAR with its partners has helped families and businesses save $360 billion on utility bills, while reducing greenhouse gas emissions by 2.5 billion metric tons since the program was implemented. ENERGY STAR continues to stay a step ahead of government code requirements and the newest technology.

ENERGY STAR certification requires inspection by independent professionals certified by the Residential Energy Services Network® (RESNET®). A special energy use rating called HERS (see "Home Energy Rating System" on p. 193) makes sure that ENERGY STAR certification meets EPA's strict energy efficiency requirements. The Westport Beach House was certified using program requirement Version 3 (in states that adopt more advanced codes, Version 3.1 is required). Today, an ENERGY STAR home uses 15% to 30% less energy than a typical new home, while delivering better comfort, quality, and durability. In 2014, about 86,000 ENERGY STAR–certified houses were built in the United States.

Beyond the label on homes, more than 70 different types of products bear the ENERGY STAR logo, including washing machines, refrigerators, dishwashers, clothes dryers, and heating and cooling equipment. For further information, visit ENERGY STAR's website (energystar.gov).

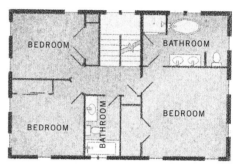

THIRD FLOOR

The Westport Beach House under construction.

Photo courtesy of Sellars Lathrop, LLC.

SECOND FLOOR

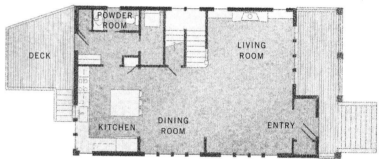

FIRST FLOOR

GREEN FEATURES
- Standing-seam recycled metal roof
- Fiber cement siding
- Low- or no-VOC paints
- Permeable paving
- Recycled materials
- Native plantings

ENERGY-EFFICIENT FEATURES
- Optimal solar orientation
- Large overhangs
- HRV
- Tankless water heater
- Radiant floor heating in bathrooms
- ENERGY STAR–rated gas heater
- Cellulose insulation
- LED and CFL lighting
- ENERGY STAR–rated appliances
- ENERGY STAR–rated ceiling fans

HOME ENERGY RATING SYSTEM (HERS)

The Home Energy Rating System is a national standard developed by RESNET, a nonprofit association that certifies energy auditors and raters as well as qualified contractors and builders. Raters perform an energy analysis of a building's design to achieve a HERS rating and then work with the builder to identify inefficiencies. RESNET auditors also suggest improvements to ensure the house will meet ENERGY STAR performance guidelines.

The HERS Index expresses the energy efficiency of a house compared to a reference house with the same dimensions, in the same climate, built according to the model energy code with a HERS Index of 100. The rating indicates how much more efficient that house is than the reference house. The lower the number, the more efficient the house. The Westport Beach House has a HERS rating of 47, which means it is 53% more efficient than the reference house. For additional information, visit the RESNET website (resnet.us).

TOP LEFT: In the second floor master bedroom, sliding barn doors for the closet were recycled from the owners' family farmhouse.

BOTTOM: With sloping ceilings and a cheery-colored end wall, the top-floor bedroom provides a cozy nook for the owner's teenage daughter.

ALPINE
PASSIVE HOUSE

Panelized

PHOTOGRAPHERS
Kristen McGaughey
(except where noted)

DESIGNER
Architrix Design Studio

BUILDER
Dürfeld Constructors

MANUFACTURER
BC Passive House

BLOWER DOOR TEST
0.33 ACH50

ENERGUIDE RATING
88

CERTIFICATIONS
Passive House (pending)

LOCATION
Whistler, B.C., Canada

SIZE
2,400 sq. ft.

ONCE VANCOUVER COUPLE SHEP AND LESLIE
Alexander became empty nesters, they began taking frequent trips to Whistler for skiing, hiking, and biking—their passions outside of work. They enjoyed shifting gears from their busy big city life to the slower pace of the mountains, and before long, they decided to move there permanently.

Their home in Vancouver was drafty and wasted energy. Their main priority in building the new house was to make it energy efficient, have a low environmental impact, and be highly durable to ensure minimal maintenance over the life of the structure.

FINDING THE BEST WAY TO BUILD

After extensive research, they decided that building a Passive House was the way to go. Their belief in resource conservation and low environmental impact drove many of the project decisions, including material and mechanical system selections, building orientation, window size and location, and space-efficient design.

After Architrix Design Studio went to work on the design, Dürfeld Constructors were hired for the building and BC Passive House was chosen to manufacture the panels. This team worked together closely to meet the Alexanders' vision of their home and the spaces inside.

MINIMIZING HEATING AND COOLING

Heating demand is the average amount of energy a house uses in a day. The space-heating energy demand of the Alpine Passive House is less than 15 kilowatts per hour per square meter per year of living space. By comparison, the typical house this size in Whistler uses 100 kilowatts per hour to 150 kilowatts per hour. Clearly, going passive provides significant savings in heating costs over the life of the building.

To achieve this level of efficiency requires a superinsulated and airtight building, smart orientation regarding the sun to help heat the building in winter, and a highly efficient heating system. The prefabricated wall panels are 10 in. thick and filled with blown-in cellulose insulation with an approximate R-value of 30. The panels were built with TJI® joists, a type of engineered wood that is stronger, straighter, and more resistant to warping, twisting, and shrinking than standard framing lumber.

To ensure an airtight building, a hybrid type panel was chosen. OSB was applied to the interior face of the wall panels, and AGEPAN® (pronounced *AH-ge-pahn*) sheathing, which is a highly vapor-permeable wood fiberboard, was used on the outside of the panels. This outer layer allows vapor that finds its way into the system to escape to the out-

Locally harvested cedar was milled into shingles and board-and-batten siding. The large overhangs protect the house from the sun in the warmer months, but during colder months when it's lower on the horizon, the sun enters, providing passive heat. Overhangs also protect the house from snow, rain, and wind. Local hemlock was used for the soffits to create visual warmth and add a welcoming approach to the home.

The open floor plan has lots of south-facing windows and is light and airy, with large doors to the outside patio. The flooring is wire-brushed oak to match the millwork. The interior window trim is local Douglas fir, and ceilings are 9 ft. tall, adding to the sense of spaciousness.

side, ensuring that the wall can breathe and stay dry. High-performance tape seals the installation at each seam.

In addition to the highly insulated and sealed exterior wall, a framed and insulated interior 2×4 "service wall" was installed to carry pipes, wires, and cables. This interior wall (which as a part of the home's structure is invisible) allows for services to run freely without interrupting the airtight OSB layer.

According to Architrix designer Khang Nguyen, the service wall is an essential part of achieving airtightness, which is key to high energy efficiency. It also makes it possible to place more insulation into the walls and reduces thermal bridging, or the transmission of heat and/or cold through the framing members, or studs, of the wall. In a typical wall, insulation is placed in between the studs; thus the studs themselves will transmit heat loss. The service wall allows for a second layer of studs and insulation in which studs are offset so no heat is lost through them.

Altogether, the exterior wall and the service wall make up the exterior thermal envelope, which is airtight and free of thermal bridging. The roof and floor panels are fabricated in a similar fashion except that roof panels are 16 in. deep with an approximate R-value of 50.

The house is heated using a highly efficient HRV, with a geothermal heat exchanger to preheat and precool the air. The geothermal exchange coils are placed in an enclosed crawl space, where the soil stays at a fairly consistent temperature year round.

Triple-pane windows are strategically placed to face south and are sized to maximize the sun's heat in the winter months. Special glazing units enable heat gain and reduce heat loss. In the summer months, when heat gain is unwanted, exterior roller screens (see "Solar Screens" on p. 199) help reduce heat by 95%.

The roof was designed to allow for the eventual installation of solar panels. It is fitted with pipes that run from the mechanical room to the roof to allow easy installation of passive hot water solar panels in the future. The entire mechanical system can be tied into that solar collection system to help supplement power.

TOP: Wide open with plenty of light and views of nature, the kitchen/dining room area neatly accommodates all the necessary functions. Kitchen cabinets are made of oak.

BOTTOM: A large picture window in the second-floor master bedroom with spectacular views toward Whistler Blackcomb Mountain, appears to bring the outside world right into the room.

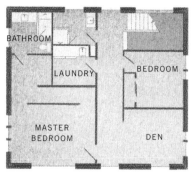

SECOND FLOOR

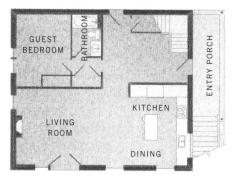

FIRST FLOOR

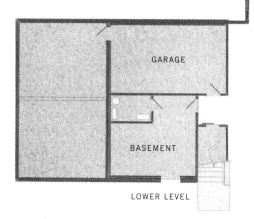

LOWER LEVEL

TOP: Views of Whistler can be seen from the south-facing patio, nestled in a landscape of native wildflowers, shrubs, and older trees that were retained when the house was built. Electrically controlled exterior solar screens are hidden within the window casing detail to create a clean facade.

BOTTOM: Panels are delivered to the site on 18-wheeler trailers with everything securely strapped into place. These panels were fabricated at the Williams Lake, B.C., facility, although a new factory has since been built in Pemberton, where BC Passive House will build panels in the future.

Photo courtesy of Khana Nguyen

GREEN FEATURES
- Shingles from locally harvested cedar
- Dual-flush toilets
- Low-VOC paint and water-based wood stains
- Garage outside the passive envelope
- Local native planting and impermeable exterior hard surfaces

ENERGY-EFFICIENT FEATURES
- Optimal orientation
- High-reflectance exterior solar roller shades on south facade
- Triple-pane windows
- Large overhangs
- Air-to-ground HRV
- Geothermal heat exchanger
- Mini-split system
- LED and CFL lighting
- ENERGY STAR–rated appliances
- ENERGY STAR–rated ceiling fans
- Solar ready

A covered walkway provides sheltered entrance to the home. It's wide enough to welcome guests, for congregating during parties, for enjoying a quiet cup of tea, and for an afternoon nap.

DESIGNED FOR COMFORTABLE LIVING

With its elegant and simple design, the house is an efficient and effective execution of Passive House requirements. Although it's not a large house, it amply provides space for comfortable living. Rooms are placed purposefully, both to ensure the best views from the most-used rooms and to provide privacy from adjacent lots and neighbors. Open, flexible-use rooms with clear sightlines to windows give the illusion of a larger space while allowing natural light to penetrate throughout the home. This also serves to light up areas that have no window access.

Not only is the Alpine Passive House supremely comfortable but it will also have much lower operating costs than other homes in the area and is optimized specifically to accommodate Shep and Leslie's lifestyle. The materials selected will prove to be timeless and durable in the mountain climate, allowing the owners to enjoy the home worry-free for years to come.

SOLAR SCREENS

When the solar window screens are lowered, they reflect the sun or absorb and then dissipate the sun's heat before it can enter the house. Screens reduce glare, heat, and ultraviolet rays and keep the house quiet when the wind outside is howling. Using screens to block the sun reduces the need for air-conditioning, thus reducing electric bills.

An electric motor raises and lowers screens by a remote control. To maximize their effectiveness, the screens are installed on the exterior of the window, and the roller mechanism is hidden within a housing above. The fabric is zippered into side tracks that guide the screen as it rolls up and down and keep the fabric in place even when the wind blows. The screens have 5% opacity, which keep out most of the sun's heat but still allows light to pass through them when in use. The solar screens used in the Alpine Passive House are made by Rainier (rainier.com/shade/solar-screens).

EMERALD HOUSE

Modular

PHOTOGRAPHERS
Tucker English
Photography (except
where noted)

ARCHITECT
Hybrid Architecture

BUILDER
Greenfab®

BLOWER DOOR TEST
2.99 ACH50

HERS INDEX
51

CERTIFICATIONS
LEED Platinum for
homes

LOCATION
Seattle, Wash.

SIZE
2,400 sq. ft.

SEATTLE HAS A VIGOROUS HOUSING MARKET WITH demand far exceeding supply. People looking for new homes are finding that existing houses are selling well above the listing price, often with bidding wars running up the cost. When the owners of Emerald House, a transplanted New York City couple, decided to move to Seattle for a change of life and pace, they researched the prefab industry as an alternative to buying an existing home in this bustling market.

PREFAB FOR HIGH PERFORMANCE

Instead of purchasing one of the city's typical 1900s Craftsman houses that would need renovating, the couple worked with Greenfab to build the modern green home they had always dreamed of owning. They became well educated on both prefab and green construction, working intensively with Greenfab to ensure that their home would be built using high-quality materials and have excellent energy performance.

Because the house's footprint is relatively small, much of the planning went into maximizing space, especially storage space, and minimizing energy consumption and other recurring costs. The home was built with an energy-efficient envelope and wired for future solar integration, so it will eventually reach net-zero energy performance. They call their home "Emerald" for several reasons: Seattle's nickname is the Emerald City, a nod to its greenery, and the house is environmentally green (of course).

TURNKEY WAS STRESS FREE

The Greenfab crew helped the couple find the property, build the house, prepare the foundation, and manage delivery. It took a total of $4^{1}/_{2}$ months to complete the house, from the time an existing building on the lot was torn down and salvaged to the time the owners received final approval from the city to move in. The house was delivered turnkey, so the only site work that was necessary was electrical and plumbing hookups, final siding, roofing, a custom open-tread staircase, and finished bamboo flooring.

The entire process was simplified to minimize the stress on the owners' daily lives. An additional benefit of building prefab in this dense urban neighborhood was that the construction process dramatically reduced the disturbance of workers on site (making noise, taking up parking space, etc.) because the project was finished considerably quicker than on-site construction would have been.

Durable fiber cement and tongue-and-groove cedar make up the siding of the Emerald House. Roofing is TPO. The 265-gal. rainwater cistern at the side of the house collects water that otherwise would be lost.

ABOVE: The flooring throughout the first floor is bamboo. A modification from the original plan, the open stair treads allow air and light to flow through the stairway.

ABOVE: A separate entrance leads to the apartment on the lower level, which includes a full kitchen, bath, living room, and bedroom and currently serves as an Airbnb. Clerestory windows add light and air without taking up a lot of wall space in this tight area.

ABOVE: Benefiting from the home's passive solar design, the master bedroom with en suite bathroom is aglow with natural light.

MAKING ALTERATIONS TO A PREDESIGNED PLAN

In partnership with Hybrid Architects, Greenfab worked with the clients to make custom design changes to their predesigned plan. To the upstairs floor plan, they added a walk-in closet and master bath with deep soaking tub and double sinks, and they modified the kitchen layout by removing an island and creating custom cabinetry space, including an appliance garage to reduce visual clutter. They added a custom media/shelf/storage center in the main living area and planned for roof access so the owners could build a roof deck at some point in the future. (Greenfab installed a roof hatch at the top of the stairs and extended a narrow open-tread staircase for access.)

The original plan called for a center island, but it was eliminated to make room for more cabinets and counter space and to leave the kitchen more open and uncluttered. Appliances are ENERGY STAR rated.

The couple also requested that the design include a built-out basement to incorporate a massage studio as well as a separate space with private entry to be rented through Airbnb®. This space has a full kitchen, bath, living room, and bedroom and has been fully booked since the owners moved in.

PREFAB COST SAVINGS

Before construction, the owners requested that Greenfab run an energy performance computer model to determine how much energy the home would consume based on the design and materi-

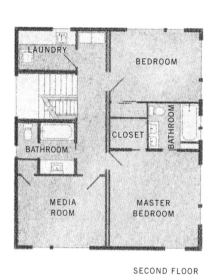
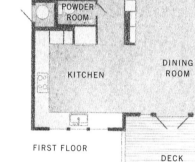
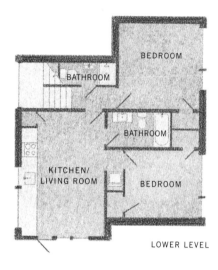

SECOND FLOOR

FIRST FLOOR

DECK

LOWER LEVEL

TOP: One of the modules under construction in the factory.

BOTTOM: The boxes on the flatbed truck ready to be delivered to the site.

Photos courtesy of Greenfab

GREEN FEATURES
- Bamboo flooring
- Dual-flush toilets
- Low-flow faucets and showers
- No-VOC interior paint
- Permeable paving
- Water infiltration pit for excess runoff
- 265-gal. rainwater cistern
- Drought-tolerant landscape

ENERGY-EFFICIENT FEATURES
- Triple-pane windows
- ERV
- Hybrid heat pump water heater
- Wall-mounted convection heaters in bedrooms
- Radiant heat mats in bathrooms
- Mini-split heat pump
- 4-in. underslab insulation
- LED lighting
- ENERGY STAR–rated appliances
- ENERGY STAR–rated ventilation

With its southern exposure, the rear of the house draws in natural light and heat, while a large cedar deck extends the interior living space into the outdoors.

als (windows, heating/cooling, fixtures, and so on) that were selected. Greenfab owner Johnny Hartsfield reports that his company "made decisions with the owners that helped improve the energy performance of their home to meet their desires to have a LEED Platinum–certified home and reduce monthly operating costs."

The total budget for the project was $585,000 (not counting the cost of the land). Included in the price was site preparation, the foundation with a full basement and rental space, and 1,700 sq. ft. of prefab home above. By prefabricating, the couple reduced their construction loan financing by $15,000 (six-month savings at $2,500/month). The project cost was $240 per square foot fully complete as compared to a custom home that typically costs a minimum of $270 per square foot in the Seattle area. This translated to approximately $72,000 in savings.

Johnny Hartsfield says his company achieves such savings because the labor costs in the factory where they produce the homes are significantly lower than where the homes are ultimately installed. In other words, the cost of living where the factory is located is far less than the cost of living in central Seattle where the house was set.

HYBRID HEAT PUMP WATER HEATER

Heat pump water heaters (HPWHs) are remarkable devices that extract heat from the surrounding air and transfer it to water stored in an enclosed tank. These systems are often referred to as *hybrids* because they can switch from efficient heat pump to standard electric heat, when fast recovery is needed during peak periods of hot water demand.

The integrated compressor and evaporator use a fan to draw in ambient heat from the surrounding air to heat refrigerant inside the compressor. The heated refrigerant then runs through coils that encircle the tank, transferring heat into the water inside the tank. According to GE®, their GeoSpring™ water heater, used in this house, reduces heating costs up to 67% over traditional electric water heaters. The control panels allow several modes of operation, which are available on most models:

Efficiency economy mode maximizes energy efficiency and savings by using only the heat pump for hot water and is the primary mode.

Auto hybrid mode is the default mode that provides energy-efficient water heating with sustained heat.

Electric heater mode is the least-energy-efficient backup mode because it uses only the electric element to heat the water.

Vacation time mode is for saving energy when the homeowner is away. The unit is put into a sleep mode until needed again.

Warmer conditions allow heat pump water heaters to operate more efficiently, while colder conditions result in slightly less efficiency. Some models offer a ducting kit to pull the heat from other areas of the house (not living spaces) and pull cold air away from the water heater location to help the unit function more efficiently. Some models also allow the homeowner to change temperature settings and modes using a smartphone. For additional information on the unit used in the Emerald House, visit GE's website (geappliances.com/heat-pump-hot-water-heater).

THREE PALMS
PROJECT

SIPs

PHOTOGRAPHER
Jake Cryan

ARCHITECT
Alliance Design

PROJECT INTERIOR
DESIGNER
Turturro Design Studio

BUILDER
Allen Construction

BLOWER DOOR TEST
0.55 ACH50

CERTIFICATIONS
LEED Platinum

SIZE
2,450 sq. ft.

THIS BEACHSIDE HOME WAS DESIGNED TO TREAD AS lightly as possible on the land and to provide an extremely healthy and energy-efficient environment. Every item and system in the house was selected with great care to meet these objectives.

ALMOST OFF THE GRID

In any house, the best way to save energy is to build an efficient exterior envelope so the house requires minimal energy. The Three Palms Project was built with SIPs for the floors, walls, and roof, which provide excellent insulation while minimizing outdoor noise. Air sealing was applied between the panels to eliminate air infiltration. The triple-pane windows used throughout the house also provide a good amount of insulation.

PV panels supply most of the energy needed for the house and can sometimes give energy back to the grid. The solar hot water panels provide hot water for household use as well as for the radiant floor heating system. Other products were selected to minimize energy use, such as ENERGY STAR–rated appliances and CFL and LED lights.

Windows and doors were designed to maximize cross ventilation, and as a result the house requires no air-conditioning system, remaining comfortable even in the warmest months. In addition, the southern side of the house has an abundance of windows to capture the beautiful ocean views and to take best advantage of the sun. The northern part of the house has fewer and smaller windows to minimize energy loss.

A HEALTHY, ECO-FRIENDLY INTERIOR ENVIRONMENT

Materials were selected to create the healthiest possible environment. According to the manufacturer, AirRenew®, the gypsum board product selected for interior walls, reduces formaldehyde released into the air and provides resistance to moisture and mildew. In addition, natural clay plaster was applied on interior walls to reduce humidity and to avoid the use of paint and other materials that might off-gas (see "Natural Plaster Walls" on p. 210).

The kitchen's GREENGUARD-certified, natural quartz countertops were chosen to eliminate VOCs and other contaminants that can be brought into the house during construction and during the life of the material. The quartz countertops are stain resistant, nonporous, and nonabsorbent. They're also harder, stronger, and easier to care for than other stone surfaces. In addition, the quartz does not require sealing with chemical-based conditioners, polishers, or wax. An ERV exchanges the air throughout the day to keep the interior air fresh while maintaining low humidity.

On the water side, the exterior wall combines fiber-reinforced cement stucco with elastomeric finishes to create a highly durable, impact-resistant, colorfast cladding. This is an effective way to seal and insulate the building envelope for energy savings.

ABOVE AND FACING PAGE TOP: All the appliances in the kitchen are ENERGY STAR rated and high efficiency, including the induction cooktop, which has a 40% faster temperature response than gas or electric. Countertops are natural and long-wearing quartz. The cabinets have a honeycomb core, which reduces raw materials by 40%. (The painting above the kitchen cabinets is *Grey Rose* by Pablo Campos.)

ABOVE: Large sliding doors and windows in the living room flood the interior with natural light. The walls have a natural plaster finish that helps regulate temperature and humidity in the house. The finished concrete floors have radiant heating, one of the most efficient ways to heat and cool a space.

NATURAL PLASTER WALLS

Natural plaster functions as an alternative to paint, which can off-gas harmful VOCs and require regular maintenance. Plaster also helps regulate interior humidity and temperature, creating a more comfortable environment. Because plaster walls absorb moisture, indoor temperatures stay at a more comfortable level, which cuts down on the need for air-conditioning.

Natural plaster is made from clay and natural aggregates and can be colored with mineral pigments. It repels dust rather than attracting it and is resistant to mold and mildew, which makes interior air quality healthier in general and specifically for people with allergies. Plaster is better for the environment because it requires minimal energy to produce and contains a large percentage of recycled materials. The material is long lasting and can be cleaned with a damp tile sponge or patched seamlessly with new plaster. A variety of pigments can be added to plaster's natural color. A white titanium, which made the walls bright white, was added to the plaster for the Three Palms Project. To learn more, visit the Naturalwalls website (naturalwalls.com) and the American Clay® website (americanclay.com).

The cabinets throughout the house are crafted with wood from sustainably managed forests and have eco-friendly finishes. The cabinets' innovative and lightweight body construction uses a high-quality, high-tech composite material that has a strong honeycomb core to reduce wood consumption (and transportation costs).

BUILDING IN HARSH WEATHER CONDITIONS

The beachside location, with its constant exposure to salt air and extreme weather conditions, made durability an important part of every design decision. Creating a low-maintenance home was an important goal.

LEFT: The addition of a car lift in the garage reduced the need for a second parking space and allowed the owners to convert what would have been garage space into 400 sq. ft. of livable square footage, now used as a media room, loft, and mechanical room.

FACING PAGE: The morning view through the large windows and sliding glass doors in the master bedroom is truly magnificent. The ENERGY STAR–rated ceiling fan keeps the room feeling comfortable. (The painting is *Azul Giorgione* by Alberto Galvez.)

BELOW: The amount of water consumed over the life of this home will be significantly reduced due to the installation of ultra-low-flow plumbing fixtures, like these in the master bath.

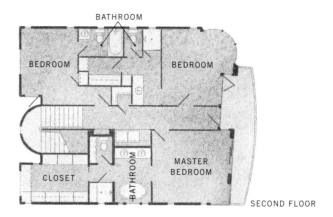

SECOND FLOOR

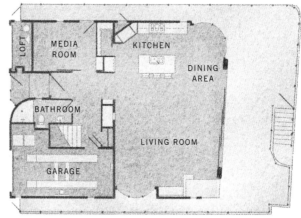

FIRST FLOOR

One of the owners' goals was to produce as much of their own energy as possible. This 5.12-kilowatt PV system provides almost all of the electricity that the house consumes. The four panels on the right are part of a solar water preheat system for both domestic hot water use and the radiant floors.

GREEN FEATURES

- Corrosion-resistant siding
- No carpeting
- Recycled and renewable materials
- Natural plaster walls
- FSC-certified wood
- GREENGUARD-certified quartz counters
- Cabinetry with FSC-certified, NAUF plywood
- Low-flow faucets and showerheads
- Dual-flush toilets
- Zero-VOC paint
- Locally sourced materials as available
- Rainwater harvesting system
- Previous house on building site recycled
- Drought-tolerant, native plantings

ENERGY-EFFICIENT FEATURES

- Passive solar orientation
- Solar panels
- PV panels
- High-efficiency windows and doors
- Daylighting
- Operable exterior shades at southern exposure
- Deep roof overhangs
- Natural cross ventilation
- ERV
- Radiant heat
- No air-conditioning
- Air sealing
- SIPs
- LED and CFL lighting throughout
- ENERGY STAR–rated appliances
- ENERGY STAR–rated ceiling fans

On the entry side, the house is covered by standing-seam titanium metal. Titanium is the only metal the architect could find that does not react or tarnish at all in the marine environment (which is why they make submarines out of it).

To this end, the homeowner chose stainless-steel railings and flashing, titanium architectural elements for their superior corrosion resistance, an acrylic stucco exterior, and metal-clad windows and doors painted with Kynar (a resin-based coating that protects against weathering and pollution).

SAVING WATER

Given the serious drought problems on the West Coast, it is essential to save water wherever and however possible. To that end, the house is equipped with a rainwater harvesting system to make use of naturally available water. Water is also conserved with dual-flush toilets and low-flow faucets on the sinks and showers.

SMART HOME ELECTRONICS

Homes are becoming more and more sophisticated and electronically integrated. Digital systems can be programmed and regulated within the home or remotely, using a smartphone or computer to control media, lighting, security, climate, pools, video, intercom, and irrigation.

The smart home control system used in the Three Palms Project allows the homeowners to automate their lighting, heating, cooling, and irrigation to maximize efficiency and conserve energy. The system can be scheduled to turn on and off at preset times, to coordinate with sunrise and sunset, or to change whenever conditions warrant, such as when temperatures drop or rise. The system can easily integrate with LED lighting systems to give the homeowners full control over the most efficient lighting options available. For more information about the system used in Three Palms Project, visit the Elan® website (elanhomesystems.com).

DAWNSKNOLL HOUSE

Panelized

PHOTOGRAPHER
Art Gray

DESIGNER/INTERIOR DESIGNER
Minarc

MANUFACTURER
mnmMOD

BUILDER
Core Construction

LOCATION
Santa Monica, Calif.

SIZE
2,500 sq. ft.

AFTER LIVING IN A CONDOMINIUM FOR 12 YEARS, THE owners of the Dawnsknoll House yearned for outdoor space in a new home in Santa Monica. The houses they saw were too large and generally were built to the edge of a lot to maximize the house size. They felt that these houses were not in "harmony with the site" and had minimal outdoor space—not what they were looking for. They wanted indoor–outdoor living along with a thoughtful way of bridging the two areas. They sought a house with clean, modern style and one that created as small a carbon footprint as possible.

After much unsuccessful house hunting, the homeowners decided to purchase a piece of land in Santa Monica and build a house designed by Minarc. The couple's aesthetics were immediately in sync with Minarc founders and principal designers, Erla Dogg Ingjaldsdottir and Tryggvi Thorsteinsson. They all agreed that the house should have limited ornamentation, a simple, clean style, and a sustainable energy-efficient design.

THE MINARC CONCEPT

Erla and Tryggvi established their company to design modern structures and to produce a panelized system that is efficient and easy to assemble. The system is manufactured locally, which eliminates waste in fabrication and during on-site construction.

Minarc houses produce no waste on site, and their construction is Cradle to Cradle Certified (see the Glossary on p. 222), energy-efficient, and has high insulation values. Simplicity is a key factor, with a limited number of assembled elements to eliminate on-site fabrication.

The exterior wall panels have a polystyrene foam core framed by galvanized steel and all wrapped in a waterproof membrane. No wood is used in the exterior walls, which are made of steel. Panels are flat packed, shipped, and assembled by as few as two workers wielding a screw gun.

BUILDING PREFAB

Building with prefabricated components appealed to the owners and it was important to them that the general contractor be familiar with prefab construction. They selected Core Construction based in part on their experience working with the mnmMOD system. Mike Stayer of Core Construction collaborated extensively with the owners (who were involved throughout design and construction), along with the Minarc design firm, the project's structural engineers, and various specialty subcontractors to come up with creative solutions and numerous unique design elements for the home.

The exterior of the house is sided with cement board and biobased wall panels. Paving is concrete, broken up by lava rock, native plants, and small patches of grass to prevent water runoff. A focal point of the house is the garage door with its facade of scrap wood and leftover quartz from the countertops—scrap that otherwise would have gone to a landfill.

ABOVE: A sliding wall system (at right) opens the house to natural light and ventilation as it expands the visual dimensions of the house. The green wall behind the television is an acoustic panel, a sound-absorbing material made entirely of recycled plastic. The steps leading up to the second floor are bamboo plywood.

LEFT: Upstairs, a bookshelf functions as a railing and barrier between the upper floor and the staircase. The white opaque sandwich panel (which is made of two translucent polycarbonate panels with a honeycomb center) to the right of the stairs encloses and provides backing for the bookshelf while allowing light through the honeycomb between panels. It's both practical and creates an interesting design when the light flows through. The light fixtures drop from the ceiling like icicles.

FACING PAGE: Furnishings in the living area include a dining table and a coffee table designed by Minarc. The pivot door that separates the office/den and living area becomes a seamlessly integrated wall when closed.

BIOBASED SIDING AND DECKING

A variety of companies make building products and construction materials from reused consumer goods that would otherwise be tossed in the garbage or landfill. TruGrain siding made with Resysta® is a biobased alternative to wood composite paneling. It has the look and feel of wood but is made of rice husks, common salt, and mineral oil combined at extremely high temperatures. The material is formed into a number of profiles and designs. Westech®, the manufacturer of TruGrain, takes agricultural waste and transforms it into a durable, sustainable building material.

TruGrain does not crack, splinter, swell, rot, or discolor. Insects don't seem to like it, making it pest and fungal resistant. It is also resistant to moisture and to the effects of saltwater, giving it a longer lifespan than wood in coastal environments. If damaged, the material can be repaired by sanding, staining, and resealing. The surface is also slip resistant, which makes it ideal for bare feet if used as decking. The manufacturer provides a 25-year warranty on residential material application of this product. For further information, visit the TruGrain website (tru-grain.com/material/what-is-trugrain).

Minarc designed the recycled rubber and scrap wood–faced powder room sink.

RUBBiSH

With more than 40.2 million reusable and waste tires generated each year in California alone (according to U.S. Rubber), Minarc decided to use some of that rubber to create useful, attractive items for the home. The company purchases the recycled rubber, which has been melted down and made into rolls. It is used to produce bathroom sinks and trim for cabinets, seating, and storage units. The product is called RUBBiSH.

A FULL-SERVICE DESIGN GROUP

Erla and Tryggvi not only helped the couple with design and building of the structure but also helped with interior and landscape design, in some cases producing several custom pieces of furniture for the house. They designed all cabinetry, most of the sinks and vanities, the coffee table and outdoor dining table, kitchen stools, and the outdoor kitchen, much of it made of RUBBiSH (see the sidebar at left).

HEATING/COOLING + SAVING ENERGY

Natural ventilation cools the house using floor-to-ceiling windows and cross ventilation. Offshore breezes from the ocean, which is about a mile away, help cool the house. Tilt-and-turn windows easily open and adjust to draw in breezes.

The house is heated with hydronic radiant floor heating. On cool days the ethanol fireplace in the living room provides all the heat they want, while also producing an attractive dancing flame (see "Bioethanol Fireplaces" on p. 221). Solar thermal panels on the roof heat the swimming pool, radiant floor, and domestic hot water. A gas heater backs up the hot water supply when required.

The house is wired for PV panels, but the couple wants to see how much energy the home consumes throughout the year before deciding how many panels to install. Because the house is built so efficiently, energy loads are low. Home electricity also powers the owners' electric car. With the combined PV and solar thermal panels, they expect the house to have a net-zero carbon footprint much of the year.

ONE PERSON'S TRASH IS ANOTHER'S TREASURE

To create the smallest carbon footprint, the owners used as many recycled and reused materials as possible in the construction. Panels used for the building envelope are Cradle to Cradle Certified. Recycled rubber was used for the powder room sink, as finish on kitchen and pantry cabinets, and on the storage/seating unit near the entry.

LEFT: Kitchen cabinets are made from bamboo plywood trimmed with a frame clad in recycled rubber. The countertops are quartz. To maximize the use of space, "disappearing" kitchen chairs easily store under the island. The blue-and-white kitchen backsplash features an illuminated photo of an Icelandic glacier taken by the owners, set onto a translucent back, and covered in fiberglass. The light fixture over the table uses polycarbonate lenses to refract and diffuse light from a single bulb.

ABOVE: The double sink in the master bathroom is built-in quartz, and the cabinets are made of bamboo plywood. A reflection of the recessed green living wall (using a hydroponic felt planting system) can be seen in the mirror for the sliding medicine cabinets.

RIGHT: Further conserving space, energy, and materials, the bedroom wall unit, made of bamboo plywood, contains a built-in bed, night tables, storage, and lights.

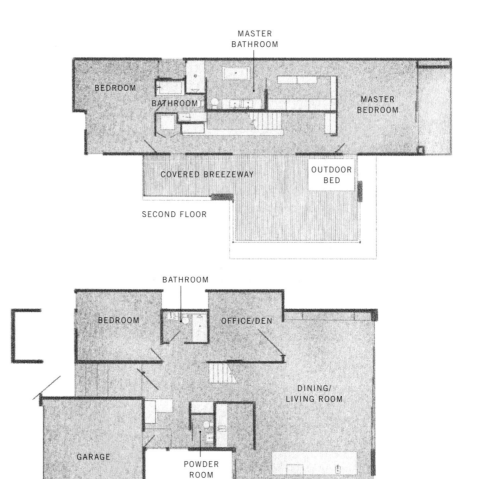

MASTER
BATHROOM

BEDROOM

BATHROOM

MASTER
BEDROOM

COVERED BREEZEWAY

OUTDOOR
BED

SECOND FLOOR

BATHROOM

BEDROOM

OFFICE/DEN

DINING/
LIVING ROOM

GARAGE

POWDER
ROOM

KITCHEN

FIRST FLOOR

Up on the second level an outdoor bed on the covered breezeway presents a grand spot for a nap. The rear decking is made from a biobased material, and the orange curtains and the cover for the outdoor bed are a natural canvaslike material that is fade and water resistant.

GREEN FEATURES

- No tiles or carpeting
- Panels built with recycled materials, Cradle to Cradle Certified
- Minimal wood use in construction process
- Sustainable FSC-certified bamboo flooring and cabinetry
- Dual-flush toilets
- No VOC finishes, dyes, or added formaldehyde
- Bioethanol fireplace
- Recycled rubber
- Reused and recycled furnishings
- Native vegetation garden (low water consumption)

ENERGY-EFFICIENT FEATURES

- Passive solar orientation
- Solar thermal panels
- Thermally broken windows and doors (see Glossary on p. 222)
- Natural ventilation (no airconditioning)
- Cross ventilation
- Radiant floor heating
- Thermally broken panel system
- LED lights throughout
- Living roof
- Energy-efficient appliances
- Induction cooktop

Much of the outdoor furniture is made from recycled materials. Outdoor dining "broom chairs" are made from discarded material found in lumberyards and industrial plastic plants, while poolside lounge chairs are made from recycled milk jugs.

For the garage door, the couple went to a custom garage door company to purchase the door mechanism. The company gave them permission to sort through their garage door scraps, which the couple then used to build the garage door facade. The final door also includes leftover pieces of quartz from the kitchen countertops as trim. Lots of trash was kept out of the landfill.

At 2,500 sq. ft., it may seem a stretch to consider this a "small" house, but for its Santa Monica location it is considerably smaller than the average local home. The Dawnsknoll House is a perfect example of form follows function and shows that the most beautiful home can be built in a thoughtful and environmentally friendly manner.

The front gate of reclaimed mixed species stacked together is visually indistinguishable from the garage door. Behind the gate, an enclosed courtyard, floating steps leading to the front door, and a water feature form an environmentally sensitive welcome. The living roof is visible above the entry facade.

BIOETHANOL FIREPLACES

Bioethanol is a renewable energy source made from formerly disposable byproducts of fermenting sugars from sugarcane, potatoes, bananas, beetroot, and more recently, cereals such as wheat. Fermenting these agricultural products produces bioethanol, a type of alcohol that is denatured to prevent human consumption (think of rubbing alcohol).

Combustion of bioethanol results in the clean emission of heat, steam, and carbon dioxide. It emits no dangerous fumes. Bioethanol fireplaces do not even require a chimney or flue, so they can be put nearly anywhere in the house and can even be taken to a new home, like furniture, when the homeowners move. Without a flue drawing the heat up and out of the house, heat from a bioethanol fireplace stays in the room. These are also easy to clean because there are no ashes or soot—only a small amount of moisture. The bioethanol fireplace in the Dawnsknoll House is from EcoSmart™ (ecosmartfire.com).

GLOSSARY

AIR SEALING

Air sealing helps to minimize drafts and air leakage through the envelope of the house. A blower door test can find where the air is leaking, and the leak can be sealed to reduce the loss of energy from the house. When the house is truly airtight, a ventilation system must be used to keep the interior air healthy and comfortable.

BLOWER DOOR TEST

A blower door test is a diagnostic tool used to measure the airtightness of a structure. A powerful fan is mounted in the frame of an exterior door. During a depressurization test, the fan pulls air out of the house, lowering the interior pressure and pulling air in from the outside through unsealed cracks and openings. A pressure gauge measures the amount of air pulled out of the house by the fan. Results of this test can determine if there are leaks in the air sealing, which can then be fixed. Properly sealing a house will increase comfort, reduce energy costs, and improve indoor air quality. This test is required for certain certification programs, including ENERGY STAR and Passive House (Passivhaus). Passive House has the most stringent blower door test requirements, allowing a maximum infiltration of 0.6 air changes per hour when measured at 50 Pascals (ACH50). Pascals are a measure of pressure. For reference, typical new houses will test between 4 ACH50 and 6 ACH50, and typical existing houses will test

between 8 ACH50 and 10 ACH50. Results below 2.0 ACH50 may be considered tight, whereas 1.0 ACH50 is a typical target for high-performance new construction.

CEILING FANS

Ceiling fans create wind that carries heat away from the body, helping to evaporate moisture from the skin and driving down body temperature. Fans churning in an empty room, however, are just wasting electricity. In warm weather, fans run counterclockwise; in cooler weather, most fans can run in reverse, forcing warm air near the ceiling down to where the people are. If used correctly, fans can lower air-conditioning and heating costs.

COOL ROOFS

Cool roofs reflect the sun's radiation and emit absorbed heat back into the atmosphere so the roof remains cooler, decreasing cooling costs and increasing comfort for the occupants. Thermoplastic polyolefin (TPO) is one of the popular cool roofing types used today. Developed by Dow® Chemical Co., TPO is a combination of rubber and hot-air-welded seams made from ethylene propylene rubber. It is resistant to tears, impact, punctures, fire, and wind uplift and is flexible enough to handle thermal expansion and contraction. Attached to the substrate material with adhesive, the roofing forms a strong chemical bond. TPO is considered an environmentally friendly material because it is recyclable, unlike

some other types of roofing materials. For further information on cool roofs, see coolroofs.org.

CRADLE TO CRADLE

Cradle to Cradle (C2C) is a design concept based on natural principles: everything is a resource for something else, use renewable energy, and celebrate diversity. Cradle to Cradle certification is a program designed to support manufacturers in a process of continuous improvement. Such companies create materials and products that cycle continuously in one of two nutrient systems: biological (things that can safely return to the soil) or technical (things that can be upcycled in perpetuity). In their 2002 book, *Cradle to Cradle: Remaking the Way We Make Things,* American designer William McDonough, in partnership with German chemist Michael Braungart, developed this concept and popularized its importance. Their program identifies products and materials that are safe for humans and the environment. The program presently has four levels of certification—basic, silver, gold, and platinum—which evaluate based on five categories: material health, material reutilization, renewable energy and carbon management, water stewardship, and social fairness. For further information about the Cradle to Cradle Certified program, see mbdc.com.

DIRECT-VENT FIREPLACES

A direct-vent fireplace does not require a chimney and can be vented through a wall or through the roof. It is one of the most efficient types of fireplaces because it draws its combustion air from outside and does not consume warm house air, as most traditional fireplaces with chimneys do. Exhaust air is expelled through concentric pipes or through separate intake and exhaust vents. This type of fireplace eliminates drafts and heat loss and does not interfere with indoor air quality. There are also vent-free fireplaces available that do not require any venting.

HEAT RECOVERY VENTILATORS AND ENERGY RECOVERY VENTILATORS

When houses are built very airtight, there can be a shortage of fresh air in the house. One popular solution is a heat recovery ventilator (HRV), which can minimize energy loss and save on heating and cooling costs. The heated or cooled conditioned interior air is exchanged with the exterior fresh air, while transferring some of the heat and coolness generated in the home. Another alternative is an energy recovery ventilator (ERV), which functions in much the same way but helps to control humidity. These are more often the ventilation choices in hot, humid climate areas. For additional information, see energy.gov/energysaver/energy-saver.

HOME ENERGY RATING SYSTEM

The Home Energy Rating System (HERS) is a national standard that was developed by RESNET, a not-for-profit association. It expresses the energy efficiency of a house compared to a reference house with the same dimensions, in the same climate, built according to the model energy code with a HERS rating of 100. A certified rating provider, working under the supervision of RESNET, determines the individual house rating. The rating is often used in determining eligibility for some programs, such as ENERGY STAR. Many older homes have a HERS rating of over 100, but many new homes are built more efficiently and are well under 100. The HERS number indicates how much more efficient that house is than the reference house, so the lower the number, the more efficient the house. For additional information about this rating, see resnet.us.

HYDRONIC AND ELECTRIC RADIANT HEATING

Radiant heat is becoming an increasingly popular heating alternative. It provides clean, even heat, warming objects in the room rather than heating the air, as forced hot air systems do. When installed correctly, radiant systems provide for greater comfort because heat is spread evenly throughout the heated area. The system can be zoned so only the areas being used are heated, increasing efficiency. Unlike forced hot air systems, with radiant heat no particulates and pollutants are forced into the environment from the blown air. In addition, the system is noise free. Radiant heating systems are embedded in flooring, ceiling, or wall panels and can even be used to melt snow on driveways and sidewalks. Hydronic or hot water radiant systems can heat a pool, a spa, and domestic hot water.

There are two types of radiant heat: electric and hydronic. Though they basically work the same way, the installations and operating costs are different. Hydronic systems are more complicated to install because they require a pump and special cross-linked polyethylene (PEX) tubing to circulate water heated by an electric, gas, or oil-fired boiler. They are easily adapted to hydronic solar panels, geothermal systems, and high-efficiency boilers because they do not require high temperatures to operate. Hydronic systems may be more expensive to install but are less expensive to operate. Electric systems are easier and less expensive to install but are more expensive to operate, making them impractical for heating an entire house but effective for small areas, such as bathrooms. One disadvantage of radiant systems is that they take longer to heat an area than other systems. Whatever material the system is embedded in acts as a heat sink, absorbing the heat first, before the room does. Depending on how big the heat sink is (such as a cold foundation), this could take quite a bit of time. On the plus side, once the heat is turned off, the heat sink will take a similarly long time to dissipate the heat, keeping the area warm for longer. To learn more, visit radiantprofessionalsalliance.org.

NO ADDED UREA FORMALDEHYDE

No Added Urea Formaldehyde (NAUF) indicates the type of resin used as a bonding agent in some wood composites. Eliminating urea formaldehyde from the bonding process improves indoor air quality.

PANELIZATION

Panelization means that the exterior and interior walls of a house and the roof and floor components are produced in a factory and then shipped to the site to be assembled like a jigsaw puzzle. Panels can include windows and doors but very often are shipped without those items already in place. Because they are built in a controlled environment, these component panels are not exposed to the elements and have less chance of later developing mold. Sophisticated machinery is often used in factories, which allows for more precise panels.

PASSIVE HOUSE

The Passive House (or Passivhaus) building energy standard, first established in Germany, is now being used in many countries around the world, including the United States. It focuses on reducing energy consumption for space heating and cooling by about 90%. The Passive House Planning Package (PHPP) is software that can be used to predict energy usage and losses for individual structures.

The requirements are stringent and include maximum heat and cooling demand, total primary energy consumption, and a maximum leakage of air volume per hour at 50 Pascals pressure, which is measured with a blower door test. Passive Houses are designed with superinsulation, high-performance windows, an airtight building shell (or envelope), and the use of an ERV to exchange the interior air with fresh outside air. Although some houses do include active solar systems, Passive Houses do not focus on producing energy but rather are designed to save approximately 75% of the entire energy used in a building compared to existing building stock. There are currently about 60,000 structures built to this standard worldwide, and it is possible for this to become the energy standard in some countries by 2020. For further information, see passivehouse.us or phius.org or passiv.de.

PERMEABLE PAVING

A variety of permeable paving materials are on the market that allow water to seep back into the ground rather than running off and collecting surface pollutants along the way. Some of these materials are porous grass pavers, gravel, crushed stone, and crushed seashells. Asphalt and concrete do not allow water to seep into the ground and generally require more maintenance than permeable materials.

R-VALUE

R-value is the measure of thermal resistance to heat flow through a given insulating material. The higher a material's R-value, the greater its insulating effectiveness. The R-value depends on the type of material, its thickness, its density, and how it is installed. If thermal bridging is created around the insulation through the studs and joists, for example, the R-value of a material can be compromised. Careful installation methods are required to achieve the maximum insulation of a structure. The amount of insulation required depends on the climate and the exposure of a particular wall. For more information, see energy.gov/energysaver/energy-saver.

ROCKWOOL INSULATION

Rockwool insulation (also known as mineral wool, slag wool, or stone wool) is made from rocks and raw minerals that are heated to about 2,910°F (1,600°C) in a furnace through which air and steam are forced, creating streams of molten minerals that cool into fibers. The molten rock can also be rotated at high speeds in a spinning wheel, spinning off fibers much the way cotton candy is made. Air pockets in the intertwined fibers trap air and hold heat. Rockwool may contain food-grade starch as a binder and oil to decrease the formation of dust. It is a good heat insulator and sound absorber, is nonirritating, and has a high fire rating. Rockwool can be blown in or made into sheets. The R-value is 2.5 per inch to 3.7 per inch.

THERMAL BRIDGING

Thermal bridging is a break in the insulation layer where heat can flow more easily from the inside of a space to the outside (or from the outside to the inside) through a material with higher conductivity or lower thermal resistance. This process can reduce the overall thermal performance of the house, leading to higher energy use and cold spots in the interior, which can cause condensation and mold. Materials that have better insulating qualities and can create a thermal break must be used to eliminate this bridge.

THERMAL MASS

Thermal mass is generally a solid substance (although it can also be a liquid) that can absorb and store warmth and coolness. Concrete, brick, and stone are examples of high-density materials that have the ability to absorb, store, and release energy back into a space. In a home, flooring, fireplaces, and walls with a high thermal mass can help to heat and cool the interior space. In winter, the solar energy is stored during the day and is released, in the form of heat, at night as the material reaches an equilibrium with the interior air. This reduces the energy required for heating the interior space. During the summer, heat is absorbed by the solid surfaces, keeping the space more comfortable during the day and reducing the need for air-conditioning.

U-VALUE OR U-FACTOR

The U-value rating represents the rate of heat transfer through building parts such as windows, doors, skylights, walls, floors, and roofs. It indicates how well these components conduct heat. A lower U-value indicates worse conduction and therefore better insulation and greater energy efficiency. A higher U-value indicates worse thermal performance. The commonly referenced R-value is simply the inverse of the U-value. The U-value is measured in units of Btus per hour per square foot per degree Fahrenheit. In lay terms, this is the rate of heat flow per square foot, per degree of temperature difference between the two sides of the material or assembly. Typical targets for high performance new construction are

- Windows: U-0.2 or less (R-5 or greater)
- Walls: U-0.03 or less (R-30 or greater)
- Roofs: U-0.02 or less (R-50 or greater)

VOLATILE ORGANIC COMPOUNDS

Paint, clear finishes, adhesives—even cleaning supplies—contain VOCs, which slowly release toxic gas into the home. Health risks from breathing VOCs include eye, nose, and throat irritation as well as liver, kidney, and central nervous system damage.

Recently, most paint companies began replacing VOCs with newer and safer ingredients. Look for interior paint certified with a Green Seal® rating for VOC content less than 50 grams per liter (g/L) for flat paint and less than 150 g/L for other finishes. Products that meet Canada's VOC standards carry their ECOLOGO® seal (a green maple leaf made up of three intertwined doves). To find out more, see.epa.gov/iaq/voc.html.

RESOURCES

CASITA DE INVIERNO

PHOTOGRAPHERS
Jeremy Scott
jeremyscottphoto.com

Rich Montalbano
rimophotographics.com

ARCHITECT/INTERIOR
DESIGNER
David Bailey / Stephanie
Harrison-Bailey

GENERAL CONTRACTOR
Sebastian Design
Implementation

SIPS SHELL BUILDER
Marquis Construction &
Development
southernsips.com

STRUCTURAL ENGINEER
Kelly E. Lyons
Alltech Structural Engineering

SUPPLIERS
Home Depot® (kitchen
cabinets)
homedepot.com

IKEA® (countertops and
furnishings)
ikea.com

L.R.E. Ground Services
(helical piers)
lregsi.com

Mitsubishi Electric® (heat
pump)
mitsubishicomfort.com

PermaTherm (SIPs)
permatherm.net

Rheem® (tankless water
heater)
rheem.com

Whirlpool® (appliances)
whirlpool.com

Windsor Windows & Doors
windsorwindows.com

EHAB CABIN

PHOTOGRAPHER
Michael Cole
michaelcolephoto.com

ARCHITECT/INTERIOR
DESIGN
Eric Cobb
Brandusa Bularca, Project
Architect
E. Cobb Architects
www.cobbarch.com

MODULAR MANUFACTURER
Dogwood Industries
dogwoodindustries.com

SITE BUILDER
Joe Hunter
Johnson & Hunter
206-352-7900

ENGINEER
Harriott Valentine Engineers
harriottvalentine.com

SUPPLIERS
Fagor (refrigerator)
fagoramerica.com

Fischer & Paykel® (range)
fisherpaykel.com/us/

The Janes Company
(in-floor heating systems)
janescompany.com

Miele® (dishwasher)
mieleusa.com

Noritz® (boiler)
noritz.com

COCOON STUDIO

PHOTOGRAPHERS
Genevieve Garruppo
genevievegarruppo.com

PREFAB DESIGN
AND BUILD
Cocoon9
cocoon9.com

ARCHITECT
Lisa R. E. Zaloga, Architects

BUILDER
Owen & Broniecki
Construction

INTERIOR DESIGNER
Sarah Storms
sarahstorms.com

STRUCTURAL ENGINEER
R&S Tavares Associates
rstavares.com

SUPPLIERS
AkzoNobel (finishes)
www.akzonobel.com

Daqsso.XTR (bamboo
exterior decking)
dassoxtr.com

Geberit (dual-flush
in-wall carrier)
geberitnorthamerica.com

Icynene® (spray foam
insulation)
icynene.com/en-us

Ignis® (ethanol fireplace)
ignisproducts.com

Mitsubishi Electric
(mini-split system)
mitsubishicomfort.com

Moen® (faucets and
shower heads)
moen.com

Novalis® (laminate flooring)
novalis-intl.com

Roca (wall-hung toilet)
roca.com

Solarban (glazing)
solarbanglasslegacy.com

Steibel Eltron (tankless
water heater)
stiebel-eltron-usa.com

Summit Appliance®
(appliances)
summitappliance.com

Sunation Solar Systems
(PV panels)
sunationsolarsystems.com

WAC Lighting® (LEDs)
waclighting.com

SANDPOINT CABIN

PHOTOGRAPHERS
Marie-Dominique Verdier
MDVphoto.com

Rob Yagid
Fine Homebuilding
finehomebuilding.com

DESIGNER
FabCab
fabcab.com

TIMBER FRAME
FraserWood Industries
fraserwoodindustries.com

SIPS
Premier Building Systems
premiersips.com

BUILDER
Selle Valley Construction
sellevalley.com

ENGINEER
John Riley
Quantum Consulting Engineers
quantumce.com

SUPPLIERS
David Trubridge
(pendant lighting)
davidtrubridge.com

Eagle® (windows and doors)
eaglewindow.com

Fagor (induction stove)
fagoramerica.com

Houzer® (sink)
houzersink.com

Liebherr (refrigerator)
liebherr-appliances.com

Mitsubishi Electric
(heat pump)
mitsubishicomfort.com

PentalQuartz® (countertop
and bathroom vanity top)
pentalquartz.com

Real Sliding Hardware
(door hardware)
realslidinghardware.com

Subway Tile Outlet
(backsplash)
subwaytileoutlet.com

Tierra Sol (floor tile)
tierrasol.ca

USFloors® (flooring)
usfloorsllc.com

Whistling Elk Woodworks
(custom cabinetry)
whistlingelkwoodworks.com

LAKESIDE CONTAINER COTTAGE

PHOTOGRAPHER
Kevin Walsh Photography
619-296-7017

ARCHITECT
obrARCHITECTURE
obrarchitecture.com

ENGINEER
Shop Engineering, Josh Gliko
shopengineering.com

SUPPLIERS
Arcadia® (windows)
arcadiainc.com

Carlisle (TPO roofing)
carlislesyntec.com

Clopay® (overhead door)
clopaydoor.com

Fantach (ERV)
fantech.net

FLOR (carpeting squares)
flor.com

IKEA (countertops and
kitchen cabinets)
ikea.com/us

James Hardie (siding)
jameshardie.com

Kohler® (fixtures)
kohler.com

LG (appliances)
lg.com/us

Mitsubichi Electric
(mini-split heat pumps)
mitsubishicomfort.com

Rheem (tankless water heater)
rheem.com

Sherwin-Williams® (paint)
sherwin-williams.com

Trex® (decking)
trex.com

Trulite® (insulating
glazing units)
trulite.com

Velux® (solar tubes)
veluxusa.com

DESERTSOL HOUSE

PHOTOGRAPHERS
Jason Flakes
jflakes.com

Kevin Duffy
kevinduffyphotography.com

MANUFACTURER
PKMM
pkmminc.com

DESIGNER/BUILDER
University of Las Vegas
students and faculty
solardecathlon.gov/past/
2013/team_lasvegas.html

SUPPLIERS
AMC Fabrication
(steel assemblies)
amcfab.com

Armstrong® (linoleum flooring)
armstrong.com

Big Ass Fans® (ceiling fans)
bigassfans.com

Bombard Renewable Energy®
(solar array installation)
bombardre.com

Bosch® (appliances)
bosch-home.com/us

Campbell® Scientific (monitors
the PV and solar thermal
systems, provides climate
data)
campbellsci.com

Centennial Woods™
(reclaimed wood siding)
centennialwoods.com

Grundfos® (domestic
water pumps)
grundfos.com

Insteon® (controls electricals,
lighting, etc.)
insteon.com

JDS Surfaces (cabinetry)
jdssurfaces.com

Kohler (plumbing fixtures)
kohler.com

Mitsubishi Electric (ductless
mini-split AC system)
mitsubishicomfort.com

NanaWall (operable windows,
glass exterior door)
nanawall.com

Uponor (piping systems)
uponor-usa.com

Viridian Reclaimed Wood
(reclaimed wood flooring)
viridianwood.com

Panasonic® (ERV)
panasonic.com

SolarUS (evacuated tube
collector system; solar hot
water panels)
solarusmfg.com

SunPower® (PV collectors
and panels)
sunpower.com

Tree Frog Veneer
treefrogveneer.com

URBANEDEN

PHOTOGRAPHER
Jason Flakes
jflakes.com

ARCHITECT/BUILDER
University of North Carolina,
Charlotte Team
urbaneden.uncc.edu

MANUFACTURER OF
WALL PANELS
Metromont
metromont.com

SUPPLIERS
Blomberg® (refrigerator)

Electrolux® (appliances)
electroluxappliances.com

Frigidaire® (convection wall
oven and dishwasher)
frigidaire.com

Ingersoll-Rand Corporation
(monitoring system)
company.ingersollrand.com

Intus Windows (windows
and doors)
intuswindows.com

Kim Lighting®
kimlighting.com

Knoll® (furnishings)
knoll.com

Lamboo® Technologies
(engineered bamboo panels)
lamboo.us

Prescolite® (lighting)
prescolite.com

Schweitzer Engineering
Laboratories® (SEL)
(programmable automation
controllers)
selinc.com

SteelFab, Inc. (steel framing)
steelfab-inc.com

Trane® (heat pumps and ERV)
trane.com

Ultra-Aire™ (dehumidifier)
ultra-aire.com

Vaughn Thermal Corporation
(heat-pump water heater)
vaughncorp.com

LAKEVIEW HOUSE

PHOTOGRAPHER
Connie J. Reinert

ARCHITECT
Domain Architecture and
Design
domainarch.com

MANUFACTURER
EPS Buildings
epsbuildings.com

SUPPLIERS
Andersen (windows
and doors)
andersenwindows.com

Heartland (vinyl siding)
proviaproducts.com/siding

Kohler (faucets)
kohler.com

LG (washer/dryer)
lg.com/us

Whirlpool (microwave)
whirlpool.com

LITTLE HOUSE ON THE FERRY

PHOTOGRAPHER
Trent Bell
trentbell.com

ARCHITECT
GO Logic
gologic.us

MANUFACTURER
Nordic
nordic.ca

ENGINEERING
Bensonwood
bensonwood.com

BUILDER
C. W. Conway and Sons
207-863-2227

INTERIOR DESIGNER
Nadja van Praag (owner)

SUPPLIERS
Arcadia (windows)
arcadiainc.com

Bosch (appliances)
bosch-home.com/us

Duravit® (bathroom fixtures)
duravit.us

IKEA (cabinets)
ikea.com/us

Hansgrohn® (faucets)
hansgrohe-usa.com

Kohler (plumbing fixtures)
kohler.com

Miele (appliances)
miele.com

Nordic (CLT panels)
nordicewp.com/products/x-lam

Viking Lumber (cedar and
framing materials)
vikinglumber.com

WAC Lighting (LED lights)
waclighting.com

SU+RE HOUSE

PHOTOGRAPHER
Juan Alicante

ARCHITECT/ BUILDER/
MANUFACTURER
2015 Solar Decathlon
team Stevens Institute of
Technology
surehouse.org

STRUCTURAL ENGINEER
Christie Engineering
www.christieengineering.com

PASSIVE HOUSE
CONSULTANTS
Building Type
bldgtyp.com

SUPPLIERS
Advanced Energy®
(solar electric PV water heater)
advanced-energy.com

Advantech
(engineered sub-flooring)
huberwood.com

BMW i3® (car)
bmw.com

Daikin® (heat pump)
daikin.com

eGauge Systems
(energy monitoring)
egauge.net

Gurit® (composite
engineering)
gurit.com

LG (solar modules)
lg.com/us

LG Hausys® (countertops)
lghausys.com

LG TurboWash™
(washer and dryer)
lg.com/us

NRG Home Solar (PV panels)
nrghomesolar.com

Pro Clima® from 475 High
Performance Building Supply
(air barrier membrane and
tapes)
proclima.com
foursevenfive.com

Renusol® (rooftop solar
racking)
renusolamerica.com

Resource Furniture
(bedroom furniture)
resourcefurniture.com

Roxul® (insulation)
roxul.com

Shüco (EAS) (windows
and doors)
schueco.com/web/us

Sika® Sarnafil® (roofing)
usa.sarnafil.sika.com
deltaroofnj.com

SMA® (solar inverter)
sma-america.com

Solbian by Pvillion
(resilient storm shutter PV)
pvilion.com
solbian.eu

TruGrain (composite
decking and louvers)
tru-grain.com

Vaughn (domestic hot
water tank)
vaughncorp.com

Zehnder (ERV)
zehnderamerica.com

BAYVIEW COTTAGE

PHOTOGRAPHER
Alison Caron Design
alisoncaron.com

ARCHITECT
Douglas Kallfelz
Union Studio
unionstudioarch.com

DEVELOPER/BUILDER
Cape Built Development
MS Ocean View

MANUFACTURER
Keiser® Homes
keisermaine.com

INTERIOR DESIGNER
Mackenzie & Mae
designedbymac.com

SUPPLIERS
Bosch (tankless water heater)
bosch-climate.us

CertainTeed® (shingles)
certainteed.com

Daltile® (flooring)
daltile.com

Heat & Glo® (mantel)
heatnglo.com

Heatilator (fireplace)
heatilator.com

Jeld-Wen® (entry door)
jeld-wen.com

Kohler (fittings)
kohler.com

Merillat® (cabinetry)
merillat.com

Mitsubishi Electric
(ductless heating and
cooling pumps)
mitsubishicomfort.com

Paradigm (impact-resistant
windows)
paradigmwindows.com

Sherwin-Williams (paint)
sherwin-williams.com

SOLAR LANEWAY HOUSE

PHOTOGRAPHER
Colin Perry
twocolumn.com

DESIGNER
Bryn Davidson
Lanefab Design/Build
lanefab.com

BUILDER
Mat Turner
Lanefab Design/Build
lanefab.com

MANUFACTURER
Insulspan® (SIPs)
insulspan.com

SUPPLIERS
Cascadia (triple-pane
windows)
cascadiawindows.com

Daikin (air source heat pump)
daikin.com

Duravit (sink)
duravit.us

Eagle (doors)
eaglewindow.com

Enphase Energy (solar
tracking)
enphase.com

Erin Pescetto (Love prints)
minted.com/store/erinpescetto

Folding Sliding Door
Company®
foldingslidingdoors.com

Future Energy Resources
(PV panels)
solarpowernrg.com

Graham & Brown® (wallpaper)
grahambrown.com

Hansgrohe (faucets)
hansgrohe-usa.com

Hay (rug)
hay.dk

Herman Miller® (office chair)
hermanmiller.com

Kohler (toilets)
kohler.com

Lotus LED (lights)
lotusledlights.com

Ola Sugden (bunny print)
olgasugden.com

Restoration Hardware®
(kitchen stools)
restorationhardware.com

Roxul (rock wool insulation)
roxul.com

Sub-Zero® (refrigerator)
subzero-wolf.com

Venmar® Eko (HRV)
venmar.ca

Watercycles (drain water
heat recovery unit)
watercycles.ca

Wolf® (stove)
subzero-wolf.com

M2 CABIN

PHOTOGRAPHER
Lannie Boesinger
lannieboesiger.wordpress.com

ARCHITECT
Balance Associates Architects
balanceassociates.com

MANUFACTURER/BUILDER
Method Homes
methodhomes.net

SUPPLIERS
CertainTeed (fiberglass
insulation)
certainteed.com/insulation

Daikin (ductless mini-split
heating and cooling system)
daikin.com

EcoTop (countertops)
kliptech.com

Modern Fan Company
(ceiling fan)
modernfan.com

Morsø (woodstove)
morsona.com

Navien® (tankless water
heater)
us.navien.com

Richlite® (paper bathroom
counters)
richlite.com

Sierra Pacific Window®
(windows and doors)
sierrapacificwindows.com

WHIDBEY ISLAND HOME

PHOTOGRAPHER
Dale Lang
nwphoto.net

ARCHITECT/MANUFACTURER
FabCab
fabcab.com

BUILDER
James Hall and Associates
jameshallandassociates.com

STRUCTURAL ENGINEER
John Riley
Quantum Consulting Engineers
quantumce.com

SUPPLIERS
Bellmont Cabinet Company
bellmontcabinets.com

Broan® (range hood)
broan.com

Eagle (windows and doors)
eaglewindow.com

Fisher & Paykel (dishwasher)
fisherpaykel.com

FLOR (carpet)
flor.com

FraserWood Industries
(timber frame)
fraserwoodindustries.com

Fujitsu® (ductless heat pump)
fujitsugeneral.com

GE (appliances)
geappliances.com

Green Depot® (bamboo
flooring)
greendepot.com

Metropolitan Appliance™
(appliances)
metropolitanappliance.com

Minka-Aire® (ceiling fans)
minkagroup.net

Panasonic (whole-house fan)
shop.panasonic.com

Premier SIPs® (SIPs)
premiersips.com

Sliding Door Company®
(sliding wall system)
slidingdoorco.com

Toto® (toilets)
totousa.com

Washington Window and Door
washingtonwindowanddoor
.com

Whirlpool (washer and dryer)
whirlpool.com

FORD HOUSE

PHOTOGRAPHER
Alison Cartwright
twisttours.com

ARCHITECT/BUILDER
KRDB/MA
krdb.com

MANUFACTURER
Palm Harbor® Homes
palmharbortx.com

SUPPLIERS
Arcadia (sliding glass doors)
arcadiainc.com

Cardinal (glass)
cardinalcorp.com

Danze® (plumbing fixtures)
danze.com

GE appliances
geappliances.com

Gerkin™ Rhino (windows)
gerkin.com

LaHabra Stucco (siding)
lahabrastucco.com

Merrilat (cabinets)
merillat.com

Rinnai (tankless water heater)
rinnai.us

Silestone® (countertops)
silestoneusa.com

SONOMA RESIDENCE

PHOTOGRAPHER
Joe Fletcher
joefletcher.com

ARCHITECT/MANUFACTURER
Connect Homes
connect-homes.com

INTERIOR DESIGNER
Meredith Rebolledo
meredithrebolledo.com

ENGINEER
R+S Tavares and Associates
rstavares.com

SUPPLIERS
Duravit (bath sink
cabinets, toilets)
duravit.us

EcoBatt insulation (insulation)
ecobatt.us

Fagor (wall oven, cooktop,
washer/dryer)
fagoramerica.com

Fisher & Paykel (dishwasher)
fisherpaykel.com

Frazee® Envirokote (paint)
brands.sherwin-williams.com/
frazee

Grohe® (faucet)
grohe.com/us

Hinkley® (exterior lights)
hinkleylighting.com

IceStone (countertops)
icestoneusa.com

IKEA (kitchen cabinets)
ikea.com

Liebherr® (refrigerator)
liebherr.us

Ma(i)sonry® (vintage furniture
and gallery)
maisonry.com

Milgard® Windows & Doors
milgard.com

Provenza (bath floor tile)
ceramicheprovenza.com

Sharp® (microwave)
sharpusa.com

Teragren® Bamboo
(wood flooring)
teragren.com

Trend (bath wall tile)
www.trend-group.com

WAC Lighting (track lighting)
waclighting.com

Western red cedar (wood
siding)
Real Cedar
realcedar.com

COUSINS RIVER
RESIDENCE

PHOTOGRAPHER
Trent Bell
trentbell.com

ARCHITECT/INTERIOR
DESIGNER
Gunther Kragler
GO Logic
gologic.us

BUILDER
Alan Gibson
GO Logic
gologic.us

STRUCTURAL ENGINEER
Albert Putnam Associates
albertputnam.com

SUPPLIERS
Amba (towel warner)
ambaproducts.com

Bega® (lighting)
bega.de/en

B-K Lighting® (lighting)
bklighting.com

CertainTeed (fiber cement
siding)
certainteed.com

Clarvista™ Glass
(glass partition)
ppgclarvistaglass.com

Design within Reach®
(coffee table and kitchen
stools)
dwr.com

District 8 (dining table)
districteightdesign.com

Duravit (bathtub)
duravit.us

Eureka (lighting)
eurekalighting.com

Grohe (faucets and
shower fixtures)
grohe.com

Kneer-Südfenster
(windows and doors)
kneer-suedfenster.de/en

Light in Art (lighting)
lightinart.com

Living Divani (sofa)
livingdivani.it

Morsø (woodstove)
morsona.com

Rich Brilliant Willing®
(lighting)
richbrilliantwilling.com

Sherwin-Williams (paint
and finishes)
sherwin-williams.com

Toto (toilets)
totousa.com

USAI® (lighting)
usailighting.com

West Elm® (rug)
westelm.com

Zehnder America (HRV)
zehnderamerica.com

WEEZERO HOUSE

ARCHITECT
Geoffrey Warner
Alchemy Architects
weehouse.com

MANUFACTURER
Irontown Homes®
irontownhomes.com

ENGINEER/CLIENT
Michael DeSutter
Ericksen Roed
eraeng.com

SUPPLIERS
Andersen (windows and doors)
andersenwindows.com

Fisher & Paykel (refrigerator)
fisherpaykel.com

IKEA (cabinetry)
ikea.com

Jenn-Air® (electric cooktop)
jennair.com

Juno® (lighting)
junolightinggroup.com

Kohler (plumbing fittings
and fixtures)
kohler.com

LG (multi-split system)
lg-dfs.com

Maax® Jazz (bathtub)
whirlpoolbathtubs.com

Teragren (bamboo floors)
teragren.com

Whirlpool (dishwasher, hood,
washer/dryer, wall oven)
whirlpool.com

CLOVERDALE HOUSE

PHOTOGRAPHER
Jamie Kowal
jaimekowal.com

ARCHITECT
Chris Pardo
Elemental Architecture
elementalarchitecture.com

MANUFACTURER/BUILDER
Method Homes
methodhomes.net

ENGINEER
Quantum Consulting Engineers
quantumce.com

SUPPLIERS
Bamboo Hardwoods®
(flooring)
bamboohardwoods.com

Big Ass Haiku (ceiling fan)
bigassfans.com

Bosch (dishwasher)
bosch-home.com/us

Daikin (mini-split)
daikin.com

Danze (bathroom faucets)
danze.com

Duravit (sinks)
duravit.us

Eagle Windows
eaglewindow.com

Frigidaire (refrigerator
and stove)
frigidaire.com

Grohe (fixtures)
hansgrohe-usa.com

LG (washer/dryer)
lg.com/us

Morsø (woodstove)
morsona.com

Panasonic (ERV)
panasonic.com

Summit Appliance
(kitchen exhaust hood)
summitappliance.com

Toto (toilet)
totousa.com

WhisperGreen Select™
(bath exhaust)
business.panasonic.com

SILICON VALLEY BALANCE HOUSE

PHOTOGRAPHER
John Swain
swainphoto.com

ARCHITECT
Claire Sheridan
Blu Homes
bluhomes.com

MANUFACTURER/BUILDER
Blu Homes
bluhomes.com

SUPPLIERS
Andersen (windows and
sliding doors)
andersenwindows.com

Artemide® (fluorescent
strip lights)
www.artemide.net

Bosch (appliances)
bosch-home.com/us

Cambria® (quartz countertops)
cambriausa.com

Florida Tile (HDP)
floridatile.com

Hampton Bay (ceiling fans)
hamptonbay-ceilingfans.com

Heat & Glo (fireplace)
heatnglo.com

Plyboo® (bamboo flooring)
plyboo.com

Sahara Furniture
(bedroom furnishings)
saharafurniture.com

Viessmann (condensing boiler)
viessmann-us.com

WAC Lighting (recessed
shower lighting)
waclighting.com

Walker Zanger® (Travertine tile
in shower)
walkerzanger.com

VASHON ISLAND HOUSE

PHOTOGRAPHER
Dale Lang
nwphoto.net

ARCHITECT
FabCab
fabcab.com

BUILDER
Greg Kruse
Potential Energy
potentialenergyinc.com

STRUCTURAL ENGINEER
John Riley
Quantum Consulting Engineers
quantumce.com

INTERIOR DESIGNER
Tamra Groh
Tamra Groh Designs

LANDSCAPE ARCHITECT
Bob Horsley
bobhorsley.com

TIMBER FRAME
FraserWood Industries
fraserwoodindustries.com

SIPS
Premier Building Systems
premiersips.com

SUPPLIERS
Benjamin Moore® (paint)
benjaminmoore.com

Eagle (windows and doors)
eaglewindow.com

Hubbardton Forge® (lighting)
hubbardtonforge.com

IKEA (cabinets)
ikea.com

Ligne Roset® (Toga sofa)
ligne-roset-usa.com

NanaWall
nanawall.com

Roche Bobois® (couch)
roche-bobois.com/en-us/

Thermolec® (tankless
water heater)
thermolec.com

VaproShield® (waterproof
roof underlayment and
weather resistant wrap)
vaproshield.com

Washington Window and Door
washingtonwindowanddoor
.com

LAKE UNION FLOATING HOME

PHOTOGRAPHER
Steve Keating
steve-keating.com

ARCHITECT
E. Cobb architects
Eric Cobb
Project architect: Jacek
Mrugala
www.cobbarch.com

STRUCTURAL ENGINEERS

Harriott Valentine Engineers
(house)
harriottvalentine.com

Swenson Say Faget, Structural
Engineers (float)
swensonsayfaget.com

BUILDER

Little and Little Construction
little-little.com

SUPPLIERS

Ann Sacks® (Carrera marble
kitchen backsplash)
annsacks.com

Benjamin Moore (paints)
benjaminmoore.com

Dornbracht® (faucets)
dornbracht.com

Duravit (sinks)
duravit.us

Fleetwood (windows)
fleetwoodusa.net

James Hardie
(fiber cement siding)
jameshardie.com

Kentwood (engineered
flooring)
kentwoodfloors.com

Kohler (bath tub)
kohler.com

Oceanside Glasstile®
(bathroom mosaic tile)
glasstile.com

PentelQuartz (countertops)
pentalquartz.com

SLV® Lighting ROX
(down lights)
slvlighting.com

Toto (toilets)
totousa.com

Vent-A-Hood® (stove vent)
ventahood.com

Wolf (stove)
subzero-wolf.com/wolf

OLDE SEAWATCH

PHOTOGRAPHER

Michael Rinko
Jump Visual
jumpvisual.com

DESIGNER

Ryan Scott Meyers
Atlantic Modular Builders
ambmodular.com

BUILDER

Atlantic Modular Builders
ambmodular.com

MANUFACTURER

Excel Homes
excelhomes.com

SUPPLIERS

Andersen (windows and doors)
andersenwindows.com

Azek® (trim)
azek.com

Brizo® (WaterSense fixtures)
brizo.com

CertainTeed (shingle siding)
certainteed.com

C.H.I. Overhead Doors®
(garage doors)
chiohd.com

DensGlass® (drywall)
buildgp.com

Heatilator (gas direct
vent fireplace)
heatilator.com

James Hardie
(ground level siding)
jameshardie.com

Merillat (cabinets)
merillat.com

Plastpro® (doors)
plastproinc.com

Ruud® (air-conditioning)
ruud.com

Ten Oaks (red oak select
hardwood floors)
tenoaksflooring.com

Timberline® HD
(roof shingles)
gaf.com

Unilock (permeable pavers)
unilock.com

HILLTOP HOUSE

PHOTOGRAPHER

Great Island Photography
greatislandphotography.com

DESIGNER

Randall Walter
Curtis Fanti
bensonwood.com

MANUFACTURER/BUILDER

Bensonwood
bensonwood.com

LANDSCAPE ARCHITECT

Daniel W. Bruzga
DB Landscaping
dblandscaping.com

SUPPLIERS

Buderus® (boiler)
bosch-climate.us

LifeBreath® (HRV)
lifebreath.com

Loewen® (windows)
loewen.com

Thermomass® (masonry
heater)
thermomass.com

Velux (skylights and
solar panels)
veluxusa.com

Vermont Custom Cabinetry™
(kitchen cabinets)
vermontcabinetry.com

Vermont Hardwoods (flooring)
vermonthardwoods.com

Vermont Soapstone
(countertops)
vermontsoapstone.com

Wolf (stove)
subzero-wolf.com/wolf

JOHNS ISLAND HOME

PHOTOGRAPHER

Margaret Rambo
rambophotography.com

ARCHITECT

Sam Rashkin
DOE Building America
Program
energy.gov/contributors/sam-
rashkin

BUILDER

Amerisips Contructors
amerisips.com

MANUFACTURER

Extreme Panel
extremepanel.com

INTERIOR DESIGNER

ABS Design Group
amerisips.com

SUPPLIERS

Andersen (windows and
sliding glass doors)
andersenwindows.com

Cali Bamboo® (flooring)
calibamboo.com

CertainTeed (lap siding
and roofing)
certainteed.com

Haas Cabinet® (kitchen
cabinets)
haascabinet.com

Heatilator (fireplace)
heatilator.com

Moen (faucets)
moen.com

PGT® (windows)
pgtindustries.com

Sherman-Williams (paint)
sherwin-williams.com

Thermador® (appliances)
thermador.com

Toto (toilets)
totousa.com

Unico (HVAC)
unicosystemgreen.com

USFloors (bamboo flooring)
usfloorsllc.com

Velux (skylights)
veluxusa.com

Viega PureFlow (water)
viega.us

HALCYON HILL

PHOTOGRAPHER

Patrick Barta Photography
bartaphoto.com

ARCHITECT/MANUFACTURER

Lindal Cedar Homes
lindal.com

ENGINEERS

Sessa Engineering Services
sessa-engineering.com

Dean Dugas
Coastructural Engineering
coasteng.ca

SUPPLIERS

Arbutus Furniture
(Murphy bed)
arbutus.com

Benjamin Moore (paint)
benjaminmoore.com

DuChâteau® (European oak
engineered flooring)
duchateau.com

IKEA (cabinets and
appliances)
ikea.com/ca/en

Logix (foundation)
logixicf.com

Robinson Lighting & Bath
Centre (lighting)
robinsonlightingandbath.com

Scan Designs (bar stools)
www.scan-design.com

Sherwin-Williams (paint)
sherwin-williams.com

Sólas (natural gas direct
vent fireplace)
solasfires.com

Whirlpool (appliances)
whirlpool.com

BONSALL HOUSE

PHOTOGRAPHERS
Daniel Hennessey
danielhennessyphotography
.com

Bryan Chan Photography
bryanchanphotography.com

ARCHITECT/MANUFACTURER
Connect Homes
connect-homes.com

BUILDER
Card Construction
(predelivery on-site work)
cardconstruction.com

SUPPLIERS
Aire-Flo® (heat pump)
aireflo-hvac.com

Americh® (bathtubs)
americh.com

Arcadia (Exterior windows
and doors)
arcadiainc.com

Caesarstone (countertops)
caesarstoneus.com

Cali Bamboo (exterior decking)
calibamboo.com

Daltile (kitchen backsplash
tile)
daltile.com

Duravit (bath, toilets)
duravit.us

EcoBatt (insulation)
ecobatt.us

EcoTimber® (wood flooring)
ecotimber.com

Fisher & Paykel (dishwasher)
fisherpaykel.com

Frazee Envirokote (paint)
brands.sherwin-williams.com/
frazee

Grohe (faucet)
grohe.com/us

Hinkley (Exterior lights)
hinkleylighting.com

IKEA (kitchen cabinets)
ikea.com/us

Majestic® (living room
gas fireplace)
majesticproducts.com

Metal Sales™ (metal siding)
metalsales.us.com

Nest Learning Thermostat
(thermostat)
nest.com

Rinnai (tankless water heater)
rinnai.us

Sharp (microwave)
sharpusa.com

Sub-Zero (refrigerator)
subzero-wolf.com

Trend (bath wall tile)
www.trend-group.com

WAC Lighting (track lighting)
waclighting.com

Wolf (range)
subzero-wolf.com

Western red cedar (wood
siding)
Real Cedar
realcedar.com

Wyndham Collection®
(bath sink cabinets)
wyndhamcollection.com

WESTPORT BEACH HOUSE

PHOTOGRAPHER
Michael Biondo
michaelbiondo.com

ARCHITECT
Sellars Lathrop Architects
sellarslathrop.com

BUILDER
The Pratley Company
pratman.com

MANUFACTURER
Bensonwood
bensonwood.com

SUPPLIERS
Azek (trim)
azek.com

Benjamin Moore (paint)
benjaminmoore.com

Feeney® (deck railing)
feeneyinc.com

Fireplace Xtrordinair®
(fireplace)
fireplacex.com

James Hardie (cementboard
siding)
jameshardie.com

Juno (lighting)
junolightinggroup.com

Lightolier® (lighting)
lightingproducts.philips.com

Marvin® Integrity®
(windows and doors)
marvin.com/integrity

Navien (tankless water heater)
us.navien.com

Schrock® (kitchen cabinets)
schrock.com

ALPINE PASSIVE HOUSE

PHOTOGRAPHER
Kristen McGaughey
www.architecturalphotos.net

DESIGNER
Architrix Design Studio
architrixstudio.com

BUILDER
Dürfeld Constructors
durfeldlogconstruction.com

ENGINEER
Equilibrium Consulting
eqcanada.com/contact

MANUFACTURER
BC Passive House
bcpassivehouse.ca

SUPPLIERS
Agepan (exterior sheathing)
agepan.de/produkt

CBR Products (exterior
staining)
cbrproducts.com

Faber® (recirculating fan
with charcoal filters)
faberonline.com

Live Edge Design® (millwork)
liveedgedesign.com

Optiwn Windows
(windows and doors)
optiwin.net

Rainier (exterior roller shades)
rainier.com/shade/solar-
screens

Siga® (air sealing tape)
sigatapes.com

Wagner™ (interior glass
railings)
wagnercompanies.com/glass_
railing.aspx

Zehnder (HRV and geothermal
heat exchanger)
zehnderamerica.com

EMERALD HOUSE

PHOTOGRAPHER
Tucker English Photography
tuckerenglishphoto.com

ARCHITECT
Hybrid Architecture
hybridarc.com

BUILDER
Greenfab
greenfab.com

ENGINEER
TSE Engineering
tse-aep.com

SUPPLIERS
Bushman™ USA
(rainwater cisterns)
bushmanusa.com

Convectair (convection
heaters)
convectair.ca/us

GE hybrid heat pump
(water heater)
geappliances.com/heat-pump-
hot-water-heater

James Hardie (siding)
jameshardie.com

Jeld-Wen (triple-pane
windows)
jeld-wen.com

Kohler (toilets)
kohler.com

LG HI-MACS® (countertops)
lghimacsusa.com

Maax (bathtubs)
maax.com/en

Mitsubishi Electric
(mini-split heating/cooling)
mitsubishicomfort.com

Moen (fixtures)
moen.com

Panasonic (WhisperComfort™
and WhisperGreen Select bath
ventilation)
business.panasonic.com

Sherman-Williams
(no-VOC paint)
sherwin-williams.com

Silestone (quartz kitchen
countertops)
silestoneusa.com

Therma-Tru® (exterior doors)
thermatru.com

THREE PALMS PROJECT

PHOTOGRAPHER
Jake Cryan
jakecryan.com

ARCHITECT
Alliance Design Group
Larry Graves
www.alliancedesigngroup.com

PROJECT DESIGNER
Turturro Design Studio
johnturturro.wix.com/
turturro-design

BUILDER
Allen Construction
buildallen.com

SUPPLIERS
AirRenew (drywall)
certainteed.com/airrenew

American Clay (clay
plaster wall finish)
americanclay.com

Bartels® (interior doors)
bartelsdoors.com

BendPak® (car lift)
bendpak.com

Bristolite® (skylights)
www.bristolite.com

Broan-NuTone® (fans)
broan-nutone.com

Cambria (quartz surfacing)
cambriausa.com

Elan (smart home electronics)
elanhomesystems.com

Forms+Surfaces® (front door)
forms-surfaces.com

Hey!Tanks LA (rainwater
harvesting system)
heytanksla.com

Icynene (insulation)
icynene.com

Kallista® (faucets)
kallista.com

Kohler (plumbing fixtures,
generator, bathtub)
kohler.com

LifeSource Water Systems®
(water treatment system)
lifesourcewater.com

Louis Poulsen® (lighting
fixtures)
louispoulsen.com

Lutron® (lighting system)
lutron.com

Natural Walls (installer of
plaster walls)
naturalwalls.com

Modern Fan (ceiling fans)
modernfan.com

Poggenpohl® (kitchen
cabinets)
poggenpohl.com

Premier SIPs (panels)
premiersips.com

Roche Bobois (Furniture)
roche-bobois.com

The Rug Affair (wool rug)
therugaffair.com

Schüco® (windows)
schueco.com

Solar Electrical Systems
(PV panels)
solarelectricalsystems.com

Sto® (acrylic stucco exterior
cladding system)
stocorp.com

Sub-Zero Wolf (appliances)
subzero-wolf.com

Targetti (lighting)
targetti.com

VividGlass (back splash)
forms-surfaces.com/vividglass

Whirlpool (appliances)
whirlpool.com

DAWNSKNOLL HOUSE

PHOTOGRAPHER
Art Gray
310-663-4756
amatgray@aol.com

ARCHITECT/MANUFACTURER
Minarc
minarc.com

BUILDER
Core Construction and
Development
18086 Mondamon Rd.
Apple Valley, CA 92307

MANUFACTURER
mnmMOD (panels)
mnmmod.com

ENGINEER
C. W. Howe
cwhowe.com

SUPPLIERS
Alinea LED lights
aamsco.com

Cem-Clad® (decorative cement
panels)
architecturalproducts.com

EcoSmart (fireplace)
ecosmartfire.com

Emeco (chairs)
emeco.net

Essentia® (outside mattress)
myessentia.com

Furin lights (icicles lights)
rotaliana.com

FSB® (hardware)
fsbna.com

Gaggenau® (appliances)
gaggenau.com

Kirei™ EchoPanel®
(acoustic panels and tiles)
kireiusa.com

KWC® (plumbing fixtures)
kwcamerica.com

Loll® Designs (lounge chairs)
lolldesigns.com

Luceplan® Hope (pendant
light)
luceplan.com

Lumisplash® (custom
illuminated backsplash)
atilaminates.com/lumisplash

Metal Window (windows and
sliding glass doors)
metalwindowcorp.com

Moxie® AIR-board®
(translucent polycarbonate
panels)
moxiesurfaces.com

Plyboo (bamboo flooring/
cabinets)
plyboo.com

Resysta (exterior finishes)
resysta.com

RUBBiSH (rubber chairs)

Silestone (countertops)
silestone.com

Sunbrella® (fabric)
eu.sunbrella.com

Teragren (bamboo cabinets)
teragren.com

Wetstyle® (bathtub)
wetstyle.ca

If you like this book, you'll love *Fine Homebuilding*.